"*Fearless Speaking* will change your life! Dr. Gary Genard gives you invaluable tools and techniques so you can stay focused, relaxed, and confident in front of an audience. You almost feel like Gary is in the room with you coaching you to success. His writing is warm, personal, caring and honest."

—JEANNIE LINDHEIM
AUTHOR OF *TRUSTING THE MOMENT:*
UNLOCKING YOUR CREATIVITY AND IMAGINATION

"This book is sensational! *Fearless Speaking* features a smart, positive method for eliminating your speaking fear immediately. You won't find a more hands-on and practical approach."

—BRAD PHILLIPS
AUTHOR, *THE MEDIA TRAINING BIBLE:*
101 THINGS YOU ABSOLUTELY, POSITIVELY NEED
TO KNOW BEFORE YOUR NEXT INTERVIEW

"A life changing book filled with 'Aha!' moments. *Fearless Speaking* is a courage-builder that will last a lifetime. It offers a clear picture of how to make our voices heard to others exactly as we intended."

—SUSAN RICE ALEXANDER
PRESIDENT/CEO, BLACK DIAMOND FRENCH TRUFFLES, INC. AND
SUSAN ALEXANDER TRUFFLES, LLC

"This book tackles the issues of speech anxiety head-on. Every speaker has some sense of lurking disaster running through his or her mind, and this is exactly what Dr. Genard addresses in *Fearless Speaking*. It's not the standard 'speak slowly, stand erect and smile at the audience' speech book. It exhaustively takes on a serious and complex issue, and delivers a comprehensive course of instruction on managing your thoughts and improving your public speaking."

—WILLIAM TICE
PRESIDENT & CEO, FRESHWEB TECHNOLOGIES INC.

"Far more effective than being told to 'relax!'"

—BRIAN PALMER
PRESIDENT, NATIONAL SPEAKERS BUREAU

"If the prospect of giving a speech fills you with dread, Gary Genard's *Fearless Speaking* is the book for you. Gary shows you how to reframe your fear and provides you with scores of tips to deal with the physical symptoms of fear that we all find so uncomfortable. A must-read for the frequent speaker."

–NICK MORGAN
PRESIDENT OF PUBLIC WORDS, INC AND AUTHOR OF
THREE BOOKS ON COMMUNICATIONS, INCLUDING *POWER CUES*,
TO BE PUBLISHED BY HARVARD IN MAY, 2014.

"Gary Genard provides the solutions to fearless public speaking because he understands our questions, doubts, roadblocks and insecurities. Gary offers a simple, eloquent, step-by-step plan for amateurs and professionals to take the stage with courage, confidence, and cool."

–ROBERT SPECTOR
AUTHOR AND INTERNATIONAL SPEAKER

"You need to be at the top of your game to succeed at public speaking. Focus, enjoyment, and passion all play a part. Dr. Gary Genard's book is the perfect recipe to help you come through loud and clear in each of those departments."

–JOSEPH KVEDAR, M.D.
FOUNDER AND DIRECTOR OF THE
CENTER FOR CONNECTED HEALTH,
PARTNERS HEALTHCARE

"Even veteran leaders can have speech anxiety despite enormous self-assurance. If that's your experience, this book can be a lifesaver. Not only does Gary Genard explain speaking fear, he offers dozens of ways to beat stage fright and demonstrate confidence. An enthusiastic thumbs-up!"

–JOHN BALDONI
EXECUTIVE COACH, AUTHOR OF *LEAD WITH PURPOSE* AND
THE LEADER'S GUIDE TO SPEAKING WITH PRESENCE

"While the shelves are filled with books on speaking, those that help people conquer fear are important. Speech anxiety keeps so many people from achieving their potential, feeling confident, and being heard. *Fearless Speaking* is practical, actionable, encouraging and empowering. What are you waiting for?"

–SUZANNE BATES
AUTHOR OF *SPEAK LIKE A CEO*

"*Fearless Speaking* is a valuable guide for anyone who gives presentations, to any audience. The self-understanding and confidence-building techniques in this book are powerful."

–JAMES ROOSEVELT, JR.
CHIEF EXECUTIVE OFFICER, TUFTS HEALTH PLAN

"Public speaking is important not only in our professional lives but also if we want to advocate for a cause. That can be nearly impossible if you have anxiety about speaking in public. *Fearless Speaking* shows you how to get out of your own way and speak from the heart. When you're that authentic you'll dig deep and your message will come through powerfully. Dr. Genard's approach will teach you how to do exactly that."

GERALDINE ACUNA
SENIOR COUNSEL, BRACEBRIDGE CAPITAL

"As a communications consultant specializing in voice, I'm very critical of others claiming to do the same thing. Imagine my delight some years ago when I discovered Gary Genard, a fellow actor who understands performance at the deepest level. Anything he writes you have to read. He really knows his stuff—and can train you fast. This book? Buy it, read it . . . do it! You won't regret it."

–FERGUS McCLELLAND
EX-FPSA. SPEAKER, COMMUNICATION CONSULTANT

FEARLESS SPEAKING

Beat Your Anxiety · Build Your Confidence · Change Your Life

GARY GENARD

Cedar &
Maitland
Press

Arlington, Massachusetts

FEARLESS SPEAKING

Cedar & Maitland Press
10 Court Street #355
Arlington, MA 02476

Orders: FearlessSpeakingBook.com
Contact: info@FearlessSpeakingBook.com

Visit our web site at www.GenardMethod.com

ISBN: 978-0-9796314-0-5
Library of Congress Control Number: 2014910964
Published in the United States of America

To my mother, Muriel Seguin.
No one had a more beautiful voice to me.

TABLE OF CONTENTS

FEARLESS SPEAKING EXERCISES

FOREWORD

How prevalent is the fear of public speaking, and is there
anything that can be done about it?

It's certainly no secret that addressing an audience brings on nervousness and anxiety in many of us. You may have heard the Jerry
Seinfeld joke, for instance, that when it comes to public speaking,
if you go to a funeral you'd be better off in the casket than doing
the eulogy. Or you may know that in 1977, the *Book of Lists* famously cited public speaking as the fear people mention more than
any other.

Whether it's treated humorously or seriously, delivering a talk has
probably been a cause of concern for as long as there has been
language and people gathered to hear it. Can we discover a way
then to become more relaxed, confident, and secure when giving a
speech—in a word, can we learn to *enjoy* it?

The answer that you'll find in these pages is a definite "Yes."

It may not surprise you to learn that the key is effective performance.

How could it be otherwise? If you're reasonably intelligent, know
your topic, and prepare sufficiently, you can conclude that you have
nothing to worry about. But fear is not a rational process; and of
course, your ability doesn't have a thing to do with whether you
experience anxiety over speaking in public. You need a way to
change your negative thinking, channel your energy, and achieve a
level of presence that matches the essence of who you are and what
you have to say.

So the question becomes: can a book help you reach those goals?

It can if it's a book on spoken *performance*.

What you're reading now is such a book, written by an actor. It examines speaking fear, *glossophobia*, entirely from the standpoint of you, the speaker, based on the type of speaking you do personally. And every one of its exercises was created to help you learn how to speak with greater ease, comfort, and confidence.

It's a complete system for transforming your anxiety into greater dynamism and enjoyment of speaking. Can it change your life, as the subtitle claims? I don't doubt it for a minute.

After all, actors aren't only superb communicators. They also know how to deal with stage fright while profoundly moving audiences. If you want to positively influence your listeners—and why else would you be speaking?—it's a vantage point you need to occupy as well.

Public speaking is a need-to-have ability for anyone in a position of authority. What you say, and how you say it, gives people a sense of the real you. A speaker who quakes on stage is not someone that others want to emulate, let alone follow. A speaker who knows the message and delivers it in a convincing manner is someone we pay attention to, not because we have to, but because we want to. Such individuals radiate authenticity. The key to authenticity is the ability to speak in your own voice in a way that draws others to you.

A wealth of information about effective public speaking awaits you in these pages: clues for understanding your speaking fear, tips on body language, tools for vocal improvement, and much more that's practical and hands-on in terms of delivery skills.

Mark Twain said that there are only two types of speakers in the world: 1. The nervous and 2. Liars.

This book will help you create an exception to that rule.

JOHN BALDONI

chair of the leadership development practice at
N2growth and author of *Lead with Purpose* and
the *Leader's Guide to Speaking with Presence*

ACKNOWLEDGMENTS

To my clients who helped me develop my methods; and to my acting colleagues who taught me about the nature of performance: a heartfelt, humble "Thank you."

Grateful acknowledgment is made to reprint the mindfulness exercises from:

The Miracle of Mindfulness by Thich Nhat Hanh
Copyright © 1975, 1976 by Thich Nhat Hanh
Preface and English translation Copyright © 1975, 1976, 1987 by Mobi Ho
Reprinted by permission of Beacon Press, Boston

DO YOU HAVE STAGE FRIGHT? A QUIZ

Please circle the appropriate number for each of your responses:

1 = STRONGLY DISAGREE 2 = DISAGREE 3 = NEUTRAL 4 = AGREE 5 = STRONGLY AGREE

LEARNED BEHAVIOR (10 QUESTIONS)

I'm comfortable speaking to small groups but uncomfortable in front of large audiences.	1	2	3	4	5
I've declined opportunities in school, career, or social groups because they involve speaking in public.	1	2	3	4	5
When I find out I'll have to give a speech or presentation, I immediately think of how I can get out of it.	1	2	3	4	5
I'm dissatisfied because I've never been able to get over my fear of public speaking.	1	2	3	4	5

I think it's better to avoid speaking altogether so people won't notice my nervousness.	1	2	3	4	5
A negative experience in the past where I experienced failure performing has stayed with me.	1	2	3	4	5
I've been unable to fully enjoy an otherwise happy occasion because I had to get up and say something.	1	2	3	4	5
I dread it when everyone around the table or the room has to introduce themselves.	1	2	3	4	5
At times I wanted to contribute to a discussion but didn't because of self-consciousness.	1	2	3	4	5
I think I'll look foolish or that people will lose respect for me if I get up to speak.	1	2	3	4	5

ANTICIPATORY ANXIETY (10 QUESTIONS)

If I have a speech or presentation coming up, I worry about it for days or weeks.	1	2	3	4	5
My sleeping habits or mood may be affected.	1	2	3	4	5
I sometimes visualize my speech or presentation going poorly prior to the engagement.	1	2	3	4	5

I tend to over-prepare my materials in case I'm caught without anything to say.	1	2	3	4	5
I'm overly concerned with how people will be thinking about my performance or me.	1	2	3	4	5
I believe that I'll come across as less knowledgeable than I really am.	1	2	3	4	5
I sometimes think I won't be as good as others who'll be speaking.	1	2	3	4	5
I worry that I'll forget what to say or won't have anything interesting to offer.	1	2	3	4	5
I'm convinced that everyone will see how nervous I am.	1	2	3	4	5
There are meetings or situations that I find particularly stressful to speak at.	1	2	3	4	5

DELIVERING YOUR SPEECH (10 QUESTIONS)

My heart starts to pound when it's time to deliver my speech or presentation.	1	2	3	4	5
I often wish I were somewhere else instead of giving this talk.	1	2	3	4	5
I experience feelings of self-consciousness or exposure when I speak in public.	1	2	3	4	5
I judge "how I'm doing" during a presentation rather than staying focused.	1	2	3	4	5

While speaking, I think people don't look interested and are judging me negatively.	1	2	3	4	5
I think the audience will sense I'm not really a leader or competent enough.	1	2	3	4	5
I'm convinced I'm physically awkward and don't use effective body language.	1	2	3	4	5
I suffer from some or all of these physical sensations: Shortness of breath, dry mouth, sweating, pounding heart, nausea, a shaky voice, or feeling hot and flushed.	1	2	3	4	5
If something goes wrong or I'm asked a tough question, I find it hard to recover and get back on track.	1	2	3	4	5
I find myself becoming preoccupied with my physical symptoms while I'm presenting.	1	2	3	4	5

SCORING:

120 – 150   **High level of stage fright.** If you're at this level, you've probably been living with an uncomfortable level of performance anxiety for some time. You probably worry about it excessively and wonder where you can find relief. *Fearless Speaking* will absolutely help you manage your speaking fear! It will "show you a way out," so you can become far more confident and comfortable speaking in public.

100 – 119   **Significant level of stage fright.** Speech anxiety is a significant part of your approach to speaking situations. You may not have made drastic life and career decisions based on your fear, but you still feel limited in your ability to enjoy speaking and to be successful at it. This book will give you a toolbox for greater control and influence when you speak to others.

70 – 99   **Moderate level of stage fright.** Some aspects of speaking in public may cause you anxiety, while others probably do not. *Fearless Speaking* will help you harness your energy, strengthen your skills in the areas in which you need improvement, and make you a more aware speaker who knows how to control a speaking situation.

Below 70   **Low level of stage fright.** You don't suffer from speaking anxiety, and you're likely a high achiever. You'd probably like to maximize your success in speeches, lectures, and presentations, however. You've come to the right place! This book will allow your influence to soar, because it will strengthen the mental, emotional, and physical aspects of your performance. Get ready to gain a wealth of valuable insight and skills for more dynamic public speaking.

CURTAIN UP!

Do you want to eliminate your fear of public speaking *forever*?

If you do, the book you're holding in your hands is the solution.

Chances are you've lived with your speech anxiety for a very long time, perhaps from your childhood. It's likely that your feelings over this issue have affected you personally and professionally. You may be avoiding speaking opportunities at work and missing out on visibility and promotions. Perhaps you're dissatisfied with your inability to stay confident and focused. Or you may go beyond ordinary nervousness to feeling miserable for days or weeks before an important presentation. It could also be true that you've wondered for years why someone as smart and capable as you are should have this problem at all.

This book will change all that.

This isn't an introductory book on public speaking, however. There are many such books on the market, some of them excellent. In fact, I wrote one myself, *How to Give a Speech* (Cedar & Maitland Press,

2007). These books offer advice about outlining and deciding on your topic, analyzing your audience, practicing, and similar issues having to do with general speaking improvement. They're valuable introductions to the world of public speaking.

Fearless Speaking is about one thing and one thing only: helping you permanently overcome any fears and anxieties about public speaking that have been holding you back and limiting your effectiveness. It offers a complete method for understanding your speaking fear, changing your negative thinking, and using positive visualization to create your own success when you speak.

And yes, it will also help reduce your nervousness while showing you how to stay focused.

It also offers more than these psychological tools. It provides you with hands-on exercises designed to make you a more comfortable and confident speaker and improve your performance. As a former stage actor in New York and London, I know that's the approach that works best to eliminate speaking anxiety and stage fright.

I specialize in such a performance-based approach that helps people become more dynamic and successful speakers. Over the years working with business people, nonprofit organizations, government employees, healthcare providers, financial professionals, lawyers, entrepreneurs, and people who speak in social situations, I developed a unique system of tools and techniques to help people come to grips with and overcome their public speaking fear.

That's the FEARLESS SPEAKING™ SYSTEM featured in this book.

By reading about this method and practicing the exercises in these pages, you'll be receiving the same valuable approaches and insights you'd experience if you came to Boston to work with me.

That's my promise to you.

THE FEARLESS SPEAKING SYSTEM

FEARLESS SPEAKING as featured in this book is a powerful **self-directed course** for eliminating your speech anxiety while strengthening your confidence and skills. It's a revolutionary approach that will dramatically boost your comfort level and competence through practical exercises and techniques. In other words it's about doing things to overcome your speaking anxiety, not just thinking or talking about them.

You can complete the entire course in as little as twelve days by focusing on one chapter per day and reading and practicing for about an hour. But you needn't complete the program in that time frame. You can spend more time on any of the exercises that you find particularly helpful—it's your choice. The FEARLESS SPEAKING SYSTEM is designed to incorporate *your* experiences and needs and to allow you to work at your own speed, as you learn powerful skills for overcoming your speaking anxiety AND PRACTICE THEM. My approach will absolutely make you a more relaxed and compelling speaker—the pace you proceed at is entirely up to you.

The important thing you need to know is this: The FEARLESS SPEAKING SYSTEM works. Every day, it's helping people just like you, from all walks of life and levels of speaking experience overcome debilitating speech anxiety to speak more productively and enjoyably.

Whether you've been shying away from speaking out socially, feeling overly self-conscious about your presentation skills, or experiencing a loss of focus or panic attacks in important speaking situations, the exercises in these pages will help, and at times amaze, you. Some of them are from the world of the theater where I spent decades performing. Others come directly from work I've done with clients over the years. Together, they represent the world's best approach for overcoming stage fright, anxiety, and excessive nervousness: concerns for millions of speakers across the globe.

Are you ready to *change your life* by eliminating your anxiety so that you can enjoy public speaking again or for the first time?

If your answer is yes, FEARLESS SPEAKING is the fear reduction system that will allow you to succeed.

THE FEARLESS SPEAKING EXERCISES

Let's face it: there's more to eliminating your speaking fear than just reading about it. You're not a talking head, after all! While you're in fear, you're likely to experience the fight-or-flight response, for instance. This produces a strong *physical* reaction. Rearranging your thought processes and emotional response to speech anxiety (a process known as cognitive restructuring) takes active hands-on work. And then there are all the aspects of body language and non-verbal communication that broadcast to audiences whether you are confident or terrified. Clearly, then, on-your-feet practical performance skills have a central role to play in reducing your stage fright and increasing your focus and effectiveness.

That's why, in addition to the emotional and intellectual approaches in these pages, you'll find plenty that's *actionable*. These valuable tips, tools, and activities are concerned with body language and movement; improving your focus and presence; and strengthening your vocal delivery so you can speak with projection and power. You'll also learn how to boost your confidence and control; to move listeners to action; and much, much more—all of it as practical as I could make it.

In other words, the FEARLESS SPEAKING SYSTEM outlined in this book will not only reduce your nervousness and apprehension, it will also give you practice at becoming a more dynamic and successful speaker.

Each chapter includes **hands-on** exercises to make that happen. There are 50 such exercises in all. Some of the invaluable techniques you'll learn include:

- Putting your fear into perspective.
- Transforming negative beliefs into positive thinking.
- Using body language and gestures to broadcast confidence.
- Positive visualizations for creating your own success as a speaker.
- Vocal skills to boost your credibility and authority.
- Biofeedback techniques to control your stress response.

- Halting a panic attack before it really starts.
- And dozens more. Each exercise incorporates *your personal experiences with speech anxiety* to help you gain skills while learning how to overcome your stage fright.

You'll also find a "Success Story" in each chapter focusing on someone who overcame their fear and improved in the abilities highlighted in that chapter.

Finally, the last chapter will get you to the point of "Learning to Love Speaking in Public"—whether you believe right now that that's possible!

I can tell you without a doubt that it is. This book, in fact, is designed to get you there, so you'll never have to ask again: "Where can I go for help?"

HOW TO USE THIS BOOK

Here's my advice for getting the most out of this book and the FEARLESS SPEAKING SYSTEM:

- Work on one chapter per day, if possible;
- Truly apply yourself to learning the new experiences you'll encounter;
- *Practice*; and
- Stay honest with yourself.

Proceed like this, and you'll make dramatic improvement in as little as 12 days, the number of chapters in the book. Or proceed more slowly—you'll end up with the same level of improvement and confidence.

* * *

Overcoming fear of public speaking is a considerable challenge. You've built up the learned behavior of speaking anxiety over years. Once you do overcome it, being a comfortable speaker brings a sense of accomplishment and sheer enjoyment that few things can equal. More than that, it opens up an entirely new world of increased visibility, the possibility of promotions, improved influence, and greater success.

Thank you for allowing *Fearless Speaking* to help get you there.

Here's wishing you more confident and enjoyable speeches and presentations!

GARY GENARD

January 19, 2014

1

UNDERSTANDING YOUR FEAR OF PUBLIC SPEAKING

The goal of this book is to change your life. To paraphrase a well-known saying: Today is the first day of the rest of your life as *someone who used to have public speaking anxiety.*

You're about to conquer a fear that has diminished your speaking pleasure, delayed your professional advancement, or disturbed your peace of mind. It may have been a nagging worry for years that you've finally decided to face, once and for all. Or perhaps your speech fright only revealed itself recently.

Some of the clients I work with, for instance, are senior executives who've been speaking in public comfortably for decades, yet they've suddenly lost their self-confidence. I don't take these clients back to their childhoods to figure out why they're anxious about speaking in public. Instead, we identify how their reluctance to speak is manifesting itself now, in the present. Once we have that information, we can work on reducing their fears and building their self-confidence along with their speaking skills.

That's exactly what this book will do for you. And you're going to get started right now. Overcoming speaking anxiety truly is something that will change your life, so why wait? Your new understanding and confidence will open up opportunities for you and show you the enjoyment you've been missing.

Just how powerful will eliminating public speaking fear be for you? The brief form below will help you decide. It's the first of many hands-on exercises for reducing speech anxiety that you'll find in *Fearless Speaking*.

EXERCISE 1-1

OVERCOMING SPEAKING ANXIETY WILL CHANGE YOUR LIFE

List three ways that not reducing but eliminating public speaking anxiety will positively impact your personal life and career:

1. _____

2. _____

3. _____

THE BEST METHOD FOR OVERCOMING YOUR SPEAKING FEAR

Obviously, the three items you just listed are important for your overall peace of mind and enjoyment of public speaking. Now, how will you actually achieve those positive developments? You probably won't be surprised to hear that the best way to overcome stage fright and reach your speaking goals is to learn a few techniques from the theater.

Actors are the world's best speakers despite speaking anxiety. Did you know, for instance, that these performers suffer from stage fright as much as anyone? The difference between actors and everyone else is that stage acting teaches them the most efficient ways for overcoming their speaking fear.

You don't need to suddenly become an actor to benefit from these techniques yourself. I do, however, use the time-tested tools and techniques of the theater with people from all walks of life because I know they produce results. I recognized this truth years ago when I began working with business executives and other professionals. After all, effective performance is the core of all good speaking—whether it's in a theater, a boardroom, a meeting, or at the conference you're attending.

Another thing that actors understand is that talking about performance is helpful only in the beginning phases of rehearsal. After that it's time for *action*.

That's why at each stage of helping people cope with their speech fear, I include **actionable exercises** to reduce apprehension while boosting my clients' skills and confidence. Some of these exercises are designed to change thinking patterns (a process known as "cognitive restructuring"). Others are based in emotional response. Some feature positive visualization, while others are concerned with staying focused and present for audiences. Whichever exercises I'm using, however, my approach always includes dealing with the body's response to stage fright. That's because fear of public speaking nearly always produces a predictable *physical* reaction.

The exercises you'll find throughout *Fearless Speaking* come directly from the approach and techniques I use in my work in Boston.

Here's the great news about the speaking jitters you experience: this level of mental and physical activation is perfectly natural and even beneficial. Without those butterflies in your stomach, you might become too laid-back and bland, without any of the edge or energy that makes you exciting as a speaker. It's only when the balance tips too far toward anxiety that the normal level of nervousness that otherwise helps you, morphs into debilitating fear.

NERVOUSNESS IS NORMAL, BUT FEAR MAKES YOU IRRATIONAL

Don't believe that those butterflies can be helpful? Then ask yourself this question: Do you know anyone who doesn't get at least a little nervous before speaking in public? I don't. I've been performing on stage since I was nine years old (my first performance was to 1,500 people). And I *still* get those butterflies before speaking to groups, and a high-stakes speech or presentation will sometimes make me have trouble sleeping the night before.

Those reactions are normal and fairly universal.

As I said earlier, stage performers undergo all of this, too. The difference is the degree of the reaction they experience. Getting slightly nervous is helpful because it psyches you up for the "big game." But deep-seated fear or a gnawing anxiety is likely to push you over into irrational thinking.

Below are four common misconceptions about public speaking that reflect such thinking. Each of them is an unreasonable conclusion, or what I call a *fiction*. You should learn to recognize them and send them on their way without you!

FOUR FICTIONS ABOUT PUBLIC SPEAKING

Fiction #1: Public speaking is dangerous. This is a particularly widespread and damaging myth. Not only are audience members not your enemy; but even a failed presentation will rarely result in your being fired, demoted, or even seriously compromised in your job. Speaking isn't a perilous adventure on the order of any of the things that should really scare you, no matter how hard you try to make it so. Remember, a diamond is formed by pressure, and only afterwards is it polished. If you find speaking in public challenging, that means it's a golden opportunity for you to shine.

Fiction #2: Nervousness will make your performance worse. There is no reliable link between feeling anxious and giving a bad performance. At least in all my years helping speakers I've never found one. Quite to the contrary, there are many stories from business and the professions, when someone will speak and then say to a colleague, "I know I was horrible . . . I was so nervous." And the other person will respond: "Really? You looked fine to me."

Fiction #3: Everyone will see how nervous you are. And once they do, the entire audience will doubt your credibility! This is nonsense. Most nervousness isn't visible to others because it's internal. And if people do see you're nervous, they'll most likely have the normal reaction, which is to sympathize with you. Since audience members feel good when you're succeeding and embarrassed when you're failing, they're actually on your side and want you to do well.

Fiction #4: You have to be an excellent speaker. Who says so? If you're a motivational speaker by profession perhaps that's so, but otherwise it isn't true. The belief that you have to be "excellent" is often a hindrance to effective public speaking because it confuses polish for true communication. When you speak to people (who almost always *want* to be in the audience), your job is to connect with them and give them something of value. Your task isn't to be slick, charismatic, or a stand-up comic. So concern yourself instead with being honest and trustworthy. And if you happen to give a lackluster presentation, so what? Failure can be the best of teachers, since you'll want to do that much better the next time.

DEVELOPING A POSITIVE MINDSET

Now that you've brought to light this quartet of damaging public speaking fictions, it's time to banish them by stepping from this negative territory into a more positive mindset. The following exercise is an excellent one for getting your thinking headed in that direction. Rather than "trying to be an excellent speaker" (as we saw above), this activity will bring you more in touch with the positive attributes you *already* have to offer listeners.

Remember, regardless of whether you succeed or fail in a particular presentation, YOUR PERFORMANCE DOESN'T CHANGE WHO YOU ARE AS A PERSON. There's an excellent reason, for instance, why you were asked to speak in front of that audience: you're exactly the right person for the job! Why not remind yourself of that fact? The exercise on the next page entitled "Your Public Speaking Strengths" is designed to help you do so.

This exercise has two parts. In the first part, you'll fill out an inventory of your attributes as a speaker. Don't be shy; be honest. This is your opportunity to reacquaint yourself with all the good things you have going for you as a presenter. It's easy to lose sight of those valuable skills once you become focused on your anxiety instead of your abilities. So for the next few minutes, blow your own trumpet . . . I won't tell!

EXERCISE 1-2

YOUR PUBLIC SPEAKING STRENGTHS

List your strengths as an oral communicator. When you're with people you feel comfortable around, what makes them listen to you? Do they appreciate your intelligence, sense of humor, passion, playfulness, kindness, quirkiness, or other traits? What assets help you when you speak to others? List your physical attributes, vocal qualities, energy, listening skills, creativity, subject matter expertise, and any other strength that helps you communicate with people.

_____

_____

_____

_____

_____

_____

_____

_____

_____

_____

_____

_____

_____

_____

_____

_____

EXERCISE 1-3

TALKING ABOUT YOUR STRENGTHS

Good! Now for the follow-through—because this is a book about better public speaking, after all.

Take a few minutes to look over your list on the previous page. Once you've become familiar with it, talk on this subject for between two and five minutes. In other words, your topic is "My Public Speaking Strengths." Use your notes if you like. Imagine that you're interviewing for a fabulous job and the interviewer says, "We're quite interested in your oral communication skills. In fact, it's the only thing we're interested in. So tell us what makes you an effective communicator."

Feel free to record your talk on audio or videotape it.

Writing down your attributes as a speaker is a down payment on your willingness to succeed at public speaking. But actually talking about good communication will give you practice in speaking freely and frequently, and get you closer to sealing the deal. So go for it!

THE BENEFITS OF STAGE FRIGHT

If your response to the above heading is, "There are actually *benefits* to stage fright?" then my answer is: You'd better believe it!

Here's why:

The anxiety you feel about important events in your life actually prepares you for challenging or dangerous situations. But as you saw in Fiction #1, public speaking *isn't* dangerous—you just perceive it that way if you have anxiety about speaking in public. Your fearful response is, therefore, a beneficial reaction that helps build up your skills so that you can succeed in front of an audience.

As I said earlier, the key is finding a *balance* between your ordinary, beneficial nervousness, and actual anxiety that's more harmful than productive.

Here are three specific ways that your "helpful" stage fright is a positive reaction:

3 WAYS STAGE FRIGHT IS HELPFUL TO YOU

1. It shows you care about your audience.

2. It gets you ready for peak performance.

3. It's a source of energy you can channel positively.

UNDERSTANDING YOUR PERSONAL RESPONSE

Now that you realize stage fright can be a positive reaction, you're ready to understand more closely your specific response to speaking fear. The step after that, later in this chapter, will be matching your reaction with the best technique to deal with that particular response.

Ready? Please turn to the exercise on the next page.

EXERCISE 1-4

UNDERSTANDING SPEAKING FEAR

Please complete the sections below concerning the eight causes of speech anxiety. Answer the questions honestly and candidly. Your answers will help you know whether you have speaking fear, and identify the type of fear response(s) you experience. Knowing this information will help you zero in on the fear reduction technique best suited to your situation.

Feel free to answer, "Yes" to more than one of the eight causes. But once you've completed the entire exercise, go back and circle the name of the response that is strongest for you. It will be helpful for you to know this information when you get to the Fear Reduction Techniques shown later in this chapter.[1]

Learned Response. *Are you still influenced by a negative public speaking or performance situation that happened to you in the past? Did something "teach" you that public appearances are unpleasant, risky, or even dangerous? Have you been afraid to get up in front of others since then?*

. . . .

Yes, I have a learned response. _____
No, I can't think of anything like that. _____
Maybe. There's something that might apply. _____
Please explain:

_____
_____
_____
_____
_____
_____
_____

---

1   For the format of this section and the Fear Reduction Techniques that follows, I am indebted to Karen Kangas Dwyer's *Conquer Your Speechfright* (Harcourt Brace 1998).

Anticipatory Anxiety. Does the thought of giving a speech or presentation cause you excessive anxiety beforehand? Do you worry constantly about the upcoming speaking situation, lose sleep, have no appetite, or fixate on what's coming?

• •

Yes, I experience excessive anticipation.   _____
No, I don't worry excessively.   _____
Somewhat.   _____
Describe what you go through:

_____

_____

_____

_____

_____

_____

_____

Mindreading. Do you believe you know what your audience is thinking? Can you "hear" them in your own mind challenging and criticizing you? Are you certain that their facial expressions reveal their true feelings toward you?

• •

Yes, I think I know what people are thinking.   _____
No, I usually leave my crystal ball at home.   _____
I respond like that in some situations.   _____
Share your thoughts with yourself now:

_____

_____

_____

_____

_____

_____

_____

Fear of Appearing Nervous. Is your greatest fear that everyone will see how nervous you are? In other words, do you think, "If I appear truly nervous, everyone will realize I don't know what I'm talking about!" Is this your big concern?

• •

Yes, I'm afraid of appearing nervous.   _____
No, I don't think like that when I'm presenting.   _____
I do worry about that at times.   _____
Please explain:

_____

_____

_____

_____

_____

_____

_____

Fear of Going Blank. Are you afraid that nervousness and anxiety will make you forget everything you're supposed to say? Do you picture yourself having a brain freeze? Are you convinced you'll be unable to say anything or that you'll forget key parts of your message?

• •

Yes, I'm constantly afraid I'll lose my train of thought.   _____
No, that isn't my concern.   _____
I sometimes have that response.   _____
Please explain these feelings:

_____

_____

_____

_____

_____

_____

_____

Lack of Skills. Are you convinced that you simply lack talent as a public speaker and shouldn't be up there? Are you afraid that you'll be "found out" and your secret will no longer be safe?

• •

Yes, I believe deep down that I'm just not a
  good speaker.   _____
No, I can't say I feel like that.   _____
Certain aspects of my speaking skills do concern me.   _____
Explain here:

_____

_____

_____

_____

_____

_____

_____

Physical Reaction. Is your biggest problem the physical responses you have when you speak in front of others? Is your principal complaint dry mouth, pounding heart, gastrointestinal distress, racing pulse, sweating, shaky voice, gasping for breath, or other symptoms?

• •

Absolutely! This is my biggest problem.   _____
No, physical distress isn't the worst thing I go through.   _____
I do experience some physical discomfort.   _____
Please explain what you feel physically if this is a source of
discomfort:

_____

_____

_____

_____

_____

_____

_____

Performance Orientation. Is your principal concern that you have to be an excellent speaker? Do you compare yourself to other speakers, telling yourself you have to come up to their level? Is your skill in performance your major concern?

• •

Yes, I need to be excellent and don't think I am. _____

No, I'm focused on my message not my performance. _____

I do sometimes compare myself with others. _____

Please explain:

_____

_____

_____

_____

_____

_____

_____

Well done! Now that you've identified possible anxiety responses, you can focus on *the technique best suited to deal with that particular response*.

Exercise 1-5 on "Types of Fear Reduction Techniques" on the next page shows you how to do that. Match the principal speaking fear you just identified (all eight are listed in the left-hand column) with the fear reduction techniques in the right column. Each of these techniques will be explained in further detail later in the book. Those are the techniques you can work closely with for maximum results![2]

---

2   Note that you needn't focus *only* on the fear reduction techniques associated with your principal response. You can also benefit from the other fear reduction techniques explained in *Fearless Speaking*, and you should pay attention to them as well.

EXERCISE 1-5

TYPES OF FEAR REDUCTION TECHNIQUES

CAUSE OF SPEECH ANXIETY	FEAR REDUCTION TECHNIQUE
Learned Response	Cognitive Restructuring (Chapter Two) Learning to Love Speaking in Public (Chapter Twelve)
Anticipatory Anxiety	Breathing Techniques (Chapter Three) Improving Focus and Presence (Chapter Five)
Mindreading	Cognitive Restructuring (Chapter Two) Using Positive Visualization (Chapter Eight)
Fear of Appearing Nervous	Body Language and Confidence (Chapter Four) Connecting with Listeners (Chapter Six)
Fear of Going Blank	Improving Focus and Presence (Chapter Five)
Lack of Skills	Connecting with Listeners (Chapter Six) Vocal Improvement (Chapter Seven)
Physical Reaction	Breathing Techniques (Chapter Three) Body Language and Confidence (Chapter Four) Biofeedback/Stress Response (Chapter Ten)
Performance Orientation	Connecting with Listeners (Chapter Six) Overcoming Extreme Self-Consciousness (Chapter Nine)

ANDREW

Andrew is a middle-aged executive with a maritime freight shipping company. He came to me because of the panic attacks he'd been experiencing when speaking at meetings. This was new to him, and he was mystified about why it was happening. He'd been a successful businessman for more than twenty years, and had always been quite comfortable speaking in public. When he experienced panic for the third time in a few weeks, he sought my help.

His response to public speaking fear was what he called a "physiological cascade": a hot wave followed by the sensation that his mouth was glued shut. Naturally, he couldn't get out the things he wanted to say. An obvious self-starter and strong personality, Andrew was determined to meet his problem head-on and defeat it.

I worked with Andrew to approach his anxiety from a different direction: not to attack it but to learn from his experiences instead. He found the relaxation exercises we practiced (you'll find them later in this book) particularly helpful. He grew easier on himself, and began to carve out quiet time to prepare when speaking at meetings and in presentations. Gradually, he realized that his "gladiatorial" approach wasn't working because he couldn't beat his anxiety into submission.

Using the relaxation techniques, Andrew gained a productive approach to dealing with his speech anxiety. And he acquired insight into how he dealt with problems generally.

2

CHANGING YOUR NEGATIVE THINKING

In Shakespeare's most famous play, Hamlet tells the character Rosencrantz: "There is nothing either good or bad, but thinking makes it so." It's a statement that is absolutely true concerning your own thoughts about your fear of public speaking.

In one sense, you create your own fearful response to public speaking. That's because, almost universally, there is never as much danger or risk as you think there is concerning a speech or presentation. However, your anxiety leads you down a path with no exit, since you're substituting your fears for more accurate measures to judge your success. So you create a false reality that's actually much harsher than the actual speaking situation.

In this chapter of *Fearless Speaking*, you'll work on changing such unprofitable thinking about speaking in public. You'll learn how to change unhealthy thoughts into constructive thinking. You'll banish the negative self-talk that's been undermining your achievements, building a repertoire of positive coping statements instead. And you'll discover how to evaluate your speaking performances more realistically, using accurate measures of your progress.

Is that a lot to accomplish in one chapter of a book? Maybe, but you'll be able to do it. That's because restructuring negative thinking is a key activity in overcoming speech anxiety—and no one knows as much about your own negative thoughts as you do.

This process, of re-routing negative thinking into productive channels is called "cognitive restructuring." For you as a presenter, it simply means going from a negative mindset to a positive one where public speaking is concerned. Another way to say this is: *you'll be changing your role from being your own worst enemy to becoming your own best friend as a speaker.*

ARE YOU BIASED AGAINST YOURSELF?

DEBORAH: A CASE STUDY

Deborah is a 36-year-old Senior Learning Manager for a leading computer manufacturer. She conducts in-house workshops worldwide for IT managers on the software that her company sells. She came to me a little less than a year ago because, she said, "I'm a horrible presenter!" Not only did she believe that she had no talent for speaking in public. She was also sure that she was broadcasting that fact to her trainees.

In Deborah's mind, it was only a matter of time before her firm's management discovered the awful truth about her lack of skills and let her go. So, she was a bundle of nerves: terrified of conducting the training workshops that were the core of her job, while to her own thinking she was "living a lie" and was constantly on the verge of being found out.

Note Deborah's response to her public speaking assignments, as described above: She *believed* that she had no talent for the task. She was *certain* everyone else realized it too. And she knew she was living a lie as a supposedly competent training professional. Clearly, Deborah's own cognitive process was a major stumbling block to her job satisfaction and feelings of self-worth!

Naturally, Deborah desperately wanted to improve what she considered inferior skills as a trainer and presenter. But as I pointed out to her, before she could get to that point, she had to change her thinking. Starting out with feelings of negative self-worth is the weakest possible position from which to build dynamic speaking skills.

* * *

Let's take Deborah's situation and apply it to the general population of people with speaking anxiety. After all, feelings like hers are common among people who believe they're simply poor speakers.

One of the biggest challenges anxious speakers like Deborah face is that they overestimate how negatively other people will judge their performance. The truth is that most audience members aren't picking apart a presenter's speaking skills. Instead, they're looking for something positive from the experience—for they want to know that attending this meeting or lecture is worth their time. In this sense, audiences actually have little interest in the speaker. They're much more focused on the message and the information being given. While that may seem a little harsh in terms of your reception from an audience, it's actually good news since you're not under as harsh a spotlight as you may have imagined!

> *Starting out with feelings of negative self-worth is the weakest possible position from which to build dynamic speaking skills.*

If you're speech phobic, you aren't aware of this, because you're too busy monitoring what you consider to be your own poor performance. *You're biased against yourself!* You may, in fact, be doing quite well, but you spoil your success by creating "a negative reality." Then you reinforce your belief that you'll do badly through self-criticism . . . even if you've actually succeeded with your goal for the speech! You might even say that you're determined to be miserable despite your success.

Does any of this sound familiar to you? If it does, you need to make the commitment *not* to indulge in self-talk that's counterproductive to successful speeches and presentations.

OVERCOMING WORST-CASE THINKING

Clearly, if, like Deborah, you indulge in a belief that you're worthless as a speaker, you need to align yourself more closely with reality. One way to do so is by overcoming *worst-case thinking*.

Worst-case thinking means imagining that a truly awful outcome is going to occur despite little or no evidence whatsoever. For instance, if the plane you're on tips to one side because of strong winds, worst-case thinking makes you wonder if one of the engines just quit. If you have a headache, worst-case thinking tells you it might be the first symptom of a brain tumor. You may be delighted to have been selected to deliver the keynote speech, but you-know-what has you thinking some rotted-out planks on the stage are going to give way just as you say, "Good evenings, ladies and gentlemen."

Ridiculous, isn't it? Yet egged on by performance anxiety, you may happily buy into such fantasies. Even if you don't really think the stage is going to collapse under you ("Well it *could!*"), you somehow believe that it might. And so in the back of your mind, you "awfulize," which is to say you welcome the most remote (and sometimes bizarre) possible outcomes.

Naturally, the reality is that such awful things rarely happen in public speaking. But worst-case thinking continues to sap your energy and keeps you focused in the wrong direction, i.e., on bad things that aren't going to happen instead of the good things that are more likely to occur.

Exercise 2-1, "Overcoming Worst-Case Thinking," is designed to point your thoughts in the right direction rather than down those dead-end alleyways.

Here's how to do the exercise:

Jot down in the first column ("Worst-Case Scenario") some really awful outcomes that you might imagine. Don't worry about being realistic—just let those wild imaginings about possible public speaking disasters out.

The next two columns are for coming back down to earth. The second column ("Actual Evidence") asks for any actual *evidence* that such catastrophes will occur. And the last column ("More Likely Outcome") prompts you to record the more probable outcome in each situation.

Go ahead . . . blast away!

EXERCISE 2-1

OVERCOMING WORST-CASE THINKING

WORST-CASE SCENARIO	ACTUAL EVIDENCE	MORE LIKELY OUTCOME

Now look over what you've got.

Is your evidence for an awful outcome on each occasion looking a bit thin?

Isn't it true that the last column—the "More Likely Outcome"—is closer to reality by a country mile? So aren't *those* the situations you should be preparing for, bringing to them a more realistic attitude and higher level of confidence?

DEVELOPING POSITIVE COPING STATEMENTS

As Exercise 2-1 demonstrates, *it's as easy to deal with reality, as it is to dwell on situations that aren't likely to occur.* The next step in cognitive restructuring is equally important. It involves changing your negative self-talk into positive coping statements.

Have you heard the term "self-fulfilling prophecy"? It means to dwell on an unpleasant or unwanted outcome so much (or so frequently) that the dreaded event comes to pass. The German philosopher Nietzsche, for instance, famously said that if you stare into the abyss long enough the abyss stares back at you. It's no different in public speaking: if you think negative thoughts consistently enough, they become your mantra. And if you're actually directing your energies toward those negative outcomes, there's a good chance that at least some of them will occur.

Creating negative self-fulfilling prophecies is a popular activity among anxious public speakers! Here's what I tell clients who exhibit this behavior: If you're going to spend time and energy dwelling on an upcoming presentation, why not think *positively* rather than negatively? You'll spend exactly the same amount of time, and it doesn't take any more effort. Which prophecy do you want to come true after all: a successful outcome or a disaster?

Exercise 2-2, "Developing Positive Coping Statements," will help get you into the right mindset. In this exercise, you'll be pairing examples of negative self-talk with more positive statements on the same issue. Some of the negative self-talk given in the first column may be actual statements you already make to yourself. If that's the case, you can immediately start using the Positive Coping Statements in the other column. Below those examples is space for your own input.

By repeating your new positive coping statements, you'll be creating a new mantra that helps you prepare not for failure but success. It's a simple yet powerful way to change your negative thinking process!

EXERCISE 2-2

DEVELOPING POSITIVE COPING STATEMENTS

NEGATIVE SELF-TALK	POSITIVE COPING STATEMENT
I'm just not a good public speaker.	I can learn to speak effectively.
They're going to see I'm nervous.	Most nervousness doesn't show.
I'm going to look like a fool.	I'll focus on my important message.
It's going to be a disaster.	I'll be as solid as I can be.
Lots of things could go wrong.	I'm prepared and ready.
This is a make-or-break situation.	If it doesn't go great, that's okay.
People will judge me.	I know what I'm talking about.
What have I gotten myself into?	What do I have to lose?
Everyone's going to be looking at me!	What an opportunity!
I know I'm going to go blank.	I can handle the unexpected.
They'll ask tough questions.	I'll admit I don't know something.
I have to be perfect.	I'll do the best job I can.

ASSESSING YOUR PROGRESS IN THIS CHAPTER

You should feel good about the pair of exercises you just completed. You're already building a "public speaking toolbox" of helpful strategies rather than negative thinking that undermines your confidence.

Let's review what you've worked on so far in Chapter Two of *Fearless Speaking*:

○ You now know how to restructure your negative thinking, with the help of two tried-and-true techniques: "Overcoming Worst-Case Thinking," and "Developing Positive Coping Statements."

○ Through these exercises, you've begun getting in touch with the reality of your speaking situations, rather than focusing on unlikely events that have little chance of occurring.

○ You're turning negative self-talk into statements that reinforce a healthy and positive attitude toward public speaking.

Now you're going to go one step further. And it's an important step. You're going to transform yourself from someone trying to survive speaking situations, into a speaker who uses self-expression as a tool for dynamic presenting. Ready? Please turn to Exercise 2-3, "Channeling Your Thinking – The 10s Exercise" on the next page.

EXERCISE 2-3

CHANNELING YOUR THINKING - THE 10S EXERCISE

This exercise features two techniques for channeling your thinking in the right direction. You'll do so by (a) taking a constructive rather than a destructive approach to public speaking; and (b) using repetition.

In "Channeling Your Thinking – The 10s Exercise," you create verbal patterns that you repeat to yourself. The patterns will be simple ones; yet, they'll take you all the way from vocalized self-doubt to preparing yourself to succeed every time you speak.

To begin, select a negative statement you typically use concerning your own speaking ability. You'll see some examples in the exercise. (Note that these statements aren't as concerned with speaking performance as Exercise 2-2 was, but with your idea of your overall abilities as a speaker.) Be honest with yourself regarding the things you actually say that undermine your confidence. Next, make that same statement less negative by softening it a bit. Finally, turn it around completely into a positive and affirming statement about your abilities.

Once you've created this sequence of three statements—negative, less negative, and positive—say the statements aloud ten times, reading across the page from left to right. Then go down to the second series of three statements and say them aloud ten times, and so on down the page.

The first three examples are already given to you. Below that, please write in your own statements.

THE 10-10-10 PATTERN

NEGATIVE STATEMENT	LESS NEGATIVE STATEMENT	POSITIVE STATEMENT
I'm a loser.	I'm not a loser.	I'm a winner.
I'm a poor speaker.	I'm not a poor speaker.	I'm a good speaker.
Audiences see I'm nervous.	Audiences can't see I'm nervous.	Audiences see I'm confident.
_____	_____	_____
_____	_____	_____
_____	_____	_____
_____	_____	_____
_____	_____	_____
_____	_____	_____
_____	_____	_____

Did you remember to say all of your sequences of three statements aloud?

Good—now you're ready to move on to the "10-10" Pattern. In this version, using the same statements you've already written, go directly from your negative statement into positive territory, eliminating the middle statement. Again, repeat each two-statement sequence aloud ten times across the page then move lower.

Once more, the first three examples are already provided.

THE 10-10 PATTERN

NEGATIVE STATEMENT	POSITIVE STATEMENT
I'm a loser.	I'm a winner.
I'm a poor speaker.	I'm a good speaker.
Audiences can see I'm nervous.	Audiences can see I'm confident.
_____	_____
_____	_____
_____	_____
_____	_____
_____	_____
_____	_____
_____	_____

Congratulations! You've not only practiced going from self-doubt about your speaking ability to positive affirmations. You've also given yourself a tool that has these further benefits:

1. *You've created positive statements (the right-hand column) that you can use as a mantra before you speak.*

2. *Hearing yourself say productive things out loud is reinforcement of a favorable mindset.*

DEFINE YOUR OBJECTIVES APART FROM YOUR ANXIETY

Let's conclude this chapter by discussing how your fear of public speaking and the measure of your success as a speaker are entirely separate matters. It's easy to confuse these two issues: thinking that just because you were nervous, your presentation had to have been a failure.

Because speaking anxiety makes you so uncomfortable, it sometimes becomes an all-consuming state of mind. That makes it easy for you to lose sight of a critically important fact: *Your goal is not to speak without anxiety it is to positively influence your audience.*

The fact is it's normal for you to get nervous to some degree when giving a speech. Your measure of success has to be how effectively you perform, not how edgy you feel when presenting. When you do something (such as speaking) well enough to succeed, that's an absolute measure, quite apart from the nervousness underlying your performance.

So why not define your objective clearly, and judge from that whether you've succeeded? Exercise 2-4, "Define Your Objective!" gives you the opportunity to do so. Here are some examples of effectively stated objectives that should help you measure your own performance:

> MY OBJECTIVE (FOR A TRAINING WORKSHOP):
> To train each participant on the new software, and make sure everyone gets the right answer on the test questions.

> MY OBJECTIVE (FOR A DEMONSTRATION):
> To demonstrate how the new seeds typically result in a 50% increase in crop yields.

> MY OBJECTIVE (FOR A PERSUASIVE SPEECH):
> To show how if the projected sales figures are met, investors should recoup their initial investment in this fund in three years.

Notice how each of these objectives uses the infinitive form of a verb: to train; to demonstrate; to show. These are *action-based words* that help define the success of the speaker's presentation in his or her own mind. Do you see how objectives like these exist entirely outside your nervousness? By using such measures, you can link your actions in your speech or presentation with an objective evaluation of whether you succeeded with your audience. Of course, soliciting input from your listeners as to whether you succeeded can be extremely helpful in this regard.

If you define your objective clearly so you will know when you accomplish it, and practice the other exercises in this chapter, you'll go a long way toward changing your negative thinking about your public speaking abilities.

Now it's your turn to practice this key preparation technique in the next exercise. Then you'll read how one of my clients succeeded in using clear objectives to accomplish his speaking goals.

EXERCISE 2-4

DEFINE YOUR OBJECTIVE!

Using the infinitive form of a verb, create an objective that will allow you to judge whether you've been successful in an upcoming speech or presentation. Remember to use an action verb!

_____

_____

_____

_____

_____

_____

GEORGE

George, the sales director at an HMO, described himself as a "wishy-washy" speaker. He was convinced that his presentations to his sales teams made him look ineffectual. Recognizing that he needed to be a leader, he nevertheless thought he lacked assertiveness and authority. So he would "plow through" his presentations, to get to the end as quickly as possible so it would all be over with.

His sales people, he was convinced, thought he wasn't up to the job. A quiet person like his father, he found it impossible to be dynamic. Why wasn't public speaking fun instead of being so painful, he wondered? He realized that this attitude of merely trying to survive meetings with his teams wasn't a formula for success.

George had developed a negative view of himself because he misunderstood his role and objective as a speaker. His sales people didn't need him to be a dynamic presenter—they needed him to be a good sales director! One reason that he experienced anticipatory anxiety and worrisome thoughts was because he was trying to be someone he wasn't by nature. His negative thinking resulted from pursuing a false goal—charisma—instead of his true goal: effectiveness in leading the sales department.

I worked with George to help him define his objectives in terms of measurable outcomes, rather than a much more vague "looking good." From there, we worked to improve his ability to think on his feet, his physical presence, and his control of the speaking situation. George learned to be more at ease by simply being himself when he talked. As a result, he became a more poised speaker, and he began to enjoy the team presentations.

3

BREATHING TECHNIQUES FOR RELAXATION AND CONTROL

in.spi.ra.tion

1. a breathing in, as of air into the lungs; inhaling. **2.** an inspiring or being inspired mentally or emotionally. **3.** an inspiring influence; any stimulus to creative thought or action (*Webster's New World Dictionary, Second College Edition*).

Surprised to hear that the first dictionary definition of "inspiration" has to do with *breathing*? Yet how appropriate: clear thinking, as well as a strong speaking voice to deliver that thinking both begin with proper breathing!

Life itself also depends on breathing, of course, but there are clear differences between "vegetative breathing" (breathing for life) and breathing for speech.

Before discussing those differences, let's look at why good breathing techniques are essential for reducing your public speaking anxiety. For some excellent reasons having to do with human anatomy, proper breathing places you in the right frame of *mind and body* to handle anxiety. This is entirely separate from your need to breathe well to maintain adequate brain function and for the control necessary to sustain speech.

Actors, who depend upon proper breathing techniques to create effective vocalization, put it this way: If you're in control of your breathing, you're ready to give a powerful performance; and if you're not in control, you aren't ready for a strong performance. That's a dramatic way of saying that breathing helps determine everything that's going on with you physically and mentally in terms of performing, including public speaking.

CALMING THE STORM OF SPEECH ANXIETY

If you struggle with public speaking anxiety, the first order of business is often quieting down the noise and inner chaos that's interfering with your comfort level and focus. Good breathing is not only ideal for getting you calm and concentrated—it's one of the few ways that you can actually reach such a state.

Think about it for just a moment, and you'll realize that a high level of anxiety is a bruising experience: you feel as though you've been beaten up mentally and physically. Add to this a loss of sleep or concentration, constant worry, the physiological toll that serious performance anxiety takes, and the results of speaking fear can be profound. In addition, the extreme loss of control you experience during stage fright can make it seem as though an electrical storm were taking place inside your brain and body!

To become a confident, directed, and dynamic speaker, you have to get this emotional and physical disturbance under control. You need to enter the *eye of the storm* where things are calm and quiet. From this peaceful center, you can heal—rejuvenating yourself and "turning down the volume" as you begin to apply appropriate coping mechanisms.

Here's a visualization that may help make this clear: Imagine a willow tree in the middle of a thunderstorm. High winds are torturing the slender branches of that tree, thrashing them violently; and the willow's wisp-like leaves make the wild movement all the more dramatic. That's what it can feel like when you lose control because of excessive nervousness and the inner chaos of extreme speech anxiety. Now visualize the *trunk* of the willow tree during the same storm: it's unmoving, stable, unaffected by anything except true hurricane-force winds.

To help you gain control of your breathing as someone who suffers from speech anxiety, imagine that your "inspiration" is like that tree trunk in the storm. Accept that your breath is steadfast and unwavering—the source of your calmness and stability.

So, when all else seems to be out of control as your anxiety spikes in a speaking situation, *remember that your breathing is your center.* You must always come back to the BREATH, for the breath is where life itself and serenity exist for you.

This chapter in *Fearless Speaking* is about getting you to that place— where relaxation and control of the speaking situation begin. This is the reliable physical starting point for giving successful, enjoyable, and memorable performances.

BREATHING NATURALLY

To breathe properly and productively for public speaking, you must practice *diaphragmatic breathing*. The term simply means breathing with the help of your diaphragm, the dome-shaped muscle located horizontally below your lungs and above your abdomen.

The natural breathing sequence of your body depends upon your diaphragm. Here's how it works:

When you inhale, your diaphragm moves downward and flattens somewhat, creating room above it for the vertically expanding lungs. As the diaphragm flattens, it pushes down on the abdominal area below it. Since the interior of the body has no spare real estate, your abdomen or "belly" has to go somewhere—which is outward.

That's why your abdominal wall moves outward as you inhale.

When you exhale, your lungs grow smaller, and your diaphragm, no longer pushed downward, can return to its relaxed dome shape. Since your belly (i.e., your abdominal area) is no longer being pushed upon from above, it too returns to its former position. Here's what it looks like:

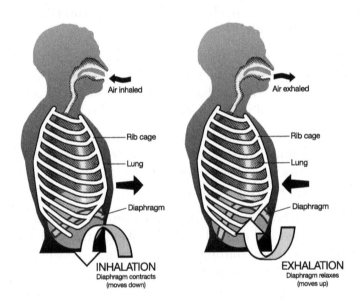

To summarize: your belly moves outward when you inhale and inward when you exhale. The classic example of this diaphragmatic action is a baby lying on its back in a crib: the baby's belly rises and falls noticeably with each inhalation-exhalation cycle.

Practicing Diaphragmatic Breathing: Try it for yourself right now. Breathe deeply and slowly and notice the movement in your abdominal area.

Does your belly move in the directions indicated above? If not—if your belly moves *inward* when you inhale—you're breathing "backwards." This reverse breathing action is actually inhibiting your diaphragmatic breathing, and can leave you short of oxygen when you speak. It's also keeping your body from breathing naturally and effortlessly, i.e., the way you need it to breathe when you're giving a speech or presentation. There's nothing inherently harmful about breathing this way; it's usually just a habit you've acquired.

Diaphragmatic breathing provides your body with an effortless and full intake of oxygen, as room is created for your lungs to expand fully. The full supply of oxygen you gain then travels from your lungs into your bloodstream, nourishing cells throughout your body. It's the perfect breathing method for a) thinking on your feet with a well oxygenated brain, and b) speaking with an authoritative and well-supported voice.

Perhaps somewhere between infancy and adulthood, however, you've developed the habit of "lazy" breathing. Add performance anxiety to the mix, and your breathing can become noticeably more rapid and shallow. As your heart rate increases due to the release of adrenaline, the negative cycle of shallow-breathing-and-rapid-heart-rate becomes locked in. Just by itself, this cycle can increase your nervousness because it makes you feel on edge, leading to more rapid shallow breathing, and so on.

If you suffer from speaking nervousness, it's critical that you re-turn to natural diaphragmatic or "belly" breathing. Doing so will slow things down, help bring you back to a state of calmness, and provide you with a full reservoir of air that will make you sound confident rather than gasping for breath.

Here are some additional benefits from proper diaphragmatic breathing:

THE 6 BENEFITS OF DIAPHRAGMATIC BREATHING

1. Slows your heart rate and centers you psychologically.

2. Provides oxygen to your brain.

3. Aids your stance and appearance.

4. Facilitates good vocal production and "the sound of authority."

5. Supports sound to the end of the sentence, where the important words come.

6. You appear confident and in control (not gasping or running out of breath).

In the following Exercise 3-1, "Progressive Relaxation," you'll learn how to release muscular tension so you can practice effortless diaphragmatic breathing. Do this exercise while lying on a yoga mat or a carpet. The first time you practice the sequence, it may take up to twenty minutes to reach the state of relaxation described. With more practice, it might take you only ten minutes to achieve the same state of full mental and physical relaxation.

EXERCISE 3-1

PROGRESSIVE RELAXATION

- Lie on your back, with eyes closed and arms and feet uncrossed at your sides.

- Follow your breath: Be aware of breathing in and out easily. "Watch" your breath as it enters your nose and goes down your throat. Stay with the nourishing breath as it passes into your lungs and then throughout your body. Feel how the oxygen nourishes every cell in your body. Become conscious of how refreshing and life affirming each miraculous breath is.

- Now, as you continue to breathe easily, focus your awareness on the top of your head. Be aware of a sense of complete relaxation: as you focus on that area, your scalp and the individual hairs on your head suddenly release all tension held within them. You feel a pleasantly heavy sensation like warm lava moving slowly down your head and scalp, gently melting away all tension as it moves.

- Allow that warm heavy feeling to spread from your scalp to your forehead. Feel the same release of tension, the melting-away, the sensation of smoothness and relaxation.

- Keeping the level of relaxation you've achieved in your scalp and forehead, let the lava flow down to your eyes. You may hold considerable tension behind your eyes—many people do. Let it melt away.

- Allow the warm melting-lava feeling to slowly proceed down your body. Each part of your body that it reaches immediately relaxes as the tension melts away. When you get to your fingers, allow any remaining tension to flow out your fingertips. And when you get to your feet, let the same thing happen through your toes. Don't DO anything; just let it happen.

- Once your body is completely relaxed, do a mental scan to locate any remaining pockets of tension. Then let that tension melt away, until you're completely and utterly relaxed. Now, allow your muscles to "remember" what this feels like, i.e., register it in your muscle memory.

- *Now that you're completely relaxed, place the palm of your dominant hand on your abdomen where it rises and falls with each breath. Breathe gently and deeply. Feel your hand moving up and down with the "bellows" action of free diaphragmatic breathing.* **This is what natural breathing in a relaxed state feels like.**

Exercise 3-1 mentions "muscle memory." Have you heard this term before? It means remembering a physical state not with your mind but with your muscles themselves. In the case of the "Progressive Relaxation" exercise, the physical state is that of complete relaxation. Such a "memory" can really come in handy when you're facing a tight moment—literally—during a talk or presentation.

In other words, at stressful moments when nervousness causes you to tighten up, muscle memory can summon up a remembered state of relaxation, helping you stay flexible and in control. With sufficient practice, you'll be able to banish at will the "freezing" effect of speaking anxiety.

The following activity, Exercise 3-2, allows you to do the same thing mentally. It's called "Mini-Vacation." It's not only the best-value vacation you'll ever find but it's also a relaxing getaway you can enjoy if you only have twenty minutes to spare!

EXERCISE 3-2

MINI-VACATION

This exercise is an excellent continuation of the benefits you gained in the previous exercise, "Progressive Relaxation." It can also be done on its own.

- Lie on your back, with your eyes closed and arms and feet uncrossed at your sides.

- Follow your breath, as in the previous exercise. Allow your body to relish each life-giving, delicious breath. Give yourself over to your breathing. Let it fill your consciousness.

- Focus your awareness on the present time and place: the here-and-now. Think about where you are. Listen to the sounds around you. Smell the air in this room. Become aware of the floor underneath you and the sensation of the air on your skin. Does this place have any taste associated with it? If you opened your eyes, what would you see? (You're using all five of your senses, of course, as you experience this time and place.) For a few minutes, fill yourself completely. Now, imagine that the reality of this place and time is dissolving, melting away into nothingness.

- In its place, you find yourself traveling to a favorite location— someplace you love to go. This place is now becoming clear in your consciousness. It might be a beach on a warm summer day, a field in springtime, a hammock outdoors in the early autumn, a cozy fire in a ski lodge at the end of a day on the slopes. Perhaps you're lying in the bottom of a rowboat that's bobbing gently at the dock. Wherever you are, this has become your new reality, and you're relaxing there.

- Open yourself up completely to this special place. Experience it sensually, with all of your senses as you did in the here-and-now. What sounds are you hearing? Seagulls? Waves slapping at the bottom of the boat? Bees buzzing? A crackling fire? Can you feel that breeze on your face as you lie in the field in the sun, or the warmth of the fire at the ski lodge? Are there any smells noticeable in this place? If you were to open your eyes, what would you see? Do you taste anything—the salty air at

the beach or the smoky air in front of the fire? Allow your senses to feed you the entirety of this world that you've recreated.

- Spend the next five or ten minutes enjoying this place. Take
  it all in deeply. Then slowly let it too begin to dissolve in your
  consciousness. In its place, bring back the present time and
  location where you're doing this exercise. And keep the level of
  deep relaxation and sensory input you've achieved. The present time and place is the same as it was before, except now
  you're experiencing it much more fully. Let it flood into you
  and throughout you.

- When you're ready, open your eyes. While staying completely
  relaxed, sit up slowly (no need to rush). Relish the sensations
  of the here and now you're still bathing in.

- Now take this feeling with you as you go about your tasks for
  the rest of the day. Keep the relaxation of your "mini-vacation"
  not only in your mind, but also in all of your senses and in your
  physical response to the world around you.

Did you notice how important your *sensory experience* was in this
exercise? Whether you were in your present location or in your
vacation spot, your world should have been filled with sensory input:
sound, smell, touch, taste, and (even with your eyes closed) the
sights of the place you were actually in or imagined you were visiting.

By the end of the exercise, you may even have achieved a new level
of awareness concerning the input of your physical senses. Good!
In a sense, you're "more alive to the world." This is a very valuable
skill to have if you're feeling isolated and removed from the present moment because of speech anxiety! Speakers who can immerse
themselves in the present and experience it fully have an invaluable
advantage concerning presence and effectiveness.

Now that you're fully relaxed physically and mentally, it's time to
practice the diaphragmatic breathing you tried only momentarily
earlier in this chapter. Exercise 3-3 will take you through the process.

EXERCISE 3-3

DIAPHRAGMATIC BREATHING

- Remember from earlier in this chapter that diaphragmatic breathing is also known as "belly breathing"? It's called this not only because the belly goes out with inhalation and back in during exhalation. The name also separates correct diaphragmatic breathing from two incorrect methods: clavicular breathing (raising the shoulder area), and thoracic breathing (thrusting out the chest). Breathing through these incorrect methods is a waste of energy, since none of the correct diaphragmatic action takes place in your chest or shoulder area!

- To begin, stand with good posture yet without tightening your torso anywhere. To breathe diaphragmatically, focus your attention on your abdominal area. This is where all of the action should take place.

- Stand easily, without tension. Place your dominant hand on your belly, i.e., at the place that goes in and out most noticeably when you breathe. That is the area of the diaphragm.

- Take relaxed deep breaths. On the inhalation, your belly "inflates" outward under your hand; on the exhalation, it returns to its former position. The movement should be easy and effortless.

- Be sure you're not "helping" your hand. Don't do anything; just breathe. Your hand will follow the natural movement of the abdominal wall that it's resting upon.

- There's no cause for concern if a huge amount of movement isn't going on down there. If you're new to diaphragmatic breathing, the action may not be too noticeable at first. The more you practice, however, the easier it will come.

- If you find that you're breathing "backwards" (see the explanation under "Practicing Diaphragmatic Breathing" earlier in this chapter), be patient. Simply observe and begin a new habit of getting the movement occurring in the right direction.

- MIRROR, MIRROR, ON THE WALL: *If you stand in front of a mirror, you'll be able to see the movement more clearly. Stand at an angle that allows you to see your belly slightly in profile. Another helpful technique is to lie in a bathtub filled with warm water. When you inhale, you'll rise noticeably in the water, just like an inner tube being inflated; and when you exhale, you'll sink back down. What an enjoyable excuse to take a relaxing bath!*

Belly breathing not only gives you a dependable supply of oxygen when you need it most in public speaking. It's also a reliable tool for keeping you calmer and more in control in *any* stressful situation. Nothing will give you less of a sense of control, on the other hand, than feeling that your breathing is out of whack, which can lead to a whole cascade of negative body sensations.

In the next chapter of *Fearless Speaking*, "Body Language to Look and Feel More Confident," you'll explore more fully this juncture of the body and effective speaking. That chapter features theater-based tools that will not only help you feel like a more confident and dynamic speaker, but equally important, look the part.

MELISSA

"When I present, I know I'm being judged," Melissa told me at our first meeting. More revealing was her next comment: "I'm just not emotionally connected with my audience. I'm protected by my designs, you see—I go into a zone when I speak and don't connect with people."

Melissa designs jewelry for a home shopping network, and she frequently showcases her work. She is very secure about her designs, but was uncomfortable talking to others and selling her ideas and vision. When it came to presentations, she found herself on autopilot, as if she were presenting in a vacuum. Or, as she said of her work (perhaps wishing that she wouldn't have to speak at all): "The designs should sell themselves."

Melissa's problem was *presence*, for she was never really in the present moment during her talks. She would speak quickly, giving almost all of her attention to the larger-than-life photos of her jewelry set up on an easel behind her. Her listeners got a much better view of the back of her head than any other part of her!

I worked with Melissa to help her become calmer and more present. She really needed to deal with the reality of her speaking engagements, and the fact that there were people in the room who were sincerely interested in her work. We focused for a considerable time on breathing, especially diaphragmatic breathing to counter her nervous shallow breaths. Melissa couldn't feel comfortable presenting her designs, because her rapid breathing didn't allow her to feel physically at ease. We also spent time on vocal issues and pacing, to bring her "down to earth" and to feel more relaxed. Slowing and deepening her breathing was the key first step, however. By breathing naturally, she could go from what felt like inner chaos, to a quieter interior space where she could feel more like herself.

4

BODY LANGUAGE TO LOOK AND FEEL MORE CONFIDENT

Whether you turn heads at the beach or consider yourself a modest physical specimen, your body is one of your most effective communication tools. Yet chances are you're not using this marvelous instrument as effectively as you could to both feel and broadcast confidence.

You probably already know that *nonverbal communication* is vital to effective public speaking, but have you ever thought about what this means apart from gestures and body positions? In fact, there's much more going on in terms of body language when you speak.

Consider the following aspects of speaking publicly that depend partly or wholly on physical expression:

- Composure
- Intention
- Self-confidence
- Emotional response
- Leadership abilities

- Self-control
- Experience
- Familiarity with presentation tools (flip charts, PowerPoint, lecterns, etc.)
- Comfort with one's material
- Vocal projection and power
- Eye contact
- Balance
- Nervousness
- Muscular tension vs. relaxation
- Extroversion vs. introversion
- Trustworthiness
- Vigor
- Fitness
- Flexibility
- Friendliness
- Openness or lack thereof
- Command of the room

If you want a reminder of how important body language and gestures are to public speaking, remember this: Every one of the attributes listed above is something that audiences can (and sometimes do) determine solely from what you demonstrate physically!

Your physical approach to public speaking, then, is completely on display at all times. Moment by moment, it's giving your audience important clues concerning who you are and what you represent. It's also alerting them to your feelings about yourself. Finally, it's telling audience members how they themselves should feel about you.

Why then do so many public speakers provide audiences with a picture that's incomplete at best and counter-productive at worst?

CONSISTENCY VS. CHANGE

Let's take a look for a moment at how body language has been portrayed in books and popular culture.

Books on body language are undoubtedly popular. Because of that popularity, they've increased awareness of the importance of nonverbal communication. At the same time, however, they've served up some erroneous information in terms of the ways in which people communicate.

How? Well, for one thing, books and articles on this topic tend to focus on reading people's behavior in social situations other than public speaking. In addition, the "rules" they set forth tend to be rigid.

Have you learned the following, for instance?

- Crossed arms means resistance.
- A woman tucking her hair behind her ears is giving positive sexual signals.
- A glance by the speaker to his or her right while answering a question signals lying.

And so on.

The truth is one-shot physical responses like those listed above mean little or nothing. Professionals whose job it is to rigorously read body language—customs officials, police interrogators, cross-examining attorneys, and so on—know that what matters more is *a change in the pattern of behavior*. In other words, when gestures, vocal quality, or the rhythm of answers suddenly differ from what's come before, a red flag pops up. The questioner or interrogator then knows to probe a little more deeply into whatever was being discussed when the new pattern of behavior began to show itself.

It's exactly the same with public speaking: The way you use your body establishes a *baseline* of your physical persona—a pattern of nonverbal messages you broadcast. Change something in that mix, and what you're showing listeners may no longer match your verbal content. Your change in physical behavior may be the result of deception; but it may as easily come from nervousness and self-consciousness about being in front of an audience. Whatever the reason, your presentation may no longer be a unified and believable whole to your audience.

All of this is why establishing a straightforward, natural, and confident persona physically will get you off to a strong and consistent start. Your body should *support* what you're saying and provide a visual expression of your content, not work in the opposite direction. Naturally, the more comfortable you are with the physical aspects of your speaking performance, the more likely it is that such a positive link between you and your material will occur.

BROADCASTING CONFIDENCE

In other words, you'll be "broadcasting" confidence.

As it happens, that's an excellent word to use in this context.

That's because visuals are as seductive in public speaking as they are in all the other aspects of our lives. Did you know, for instance, that Americans spend *eight hours a day* in front of a screen of some kind: television, computer, cell phone, tablet, e-reader, and so on?[3] Because of this fact and other ways today's audiences have been trained to be visual learners, your audience will respond most strongly to messages that you deliver in visual terms.

"Visuals" in this sense doesn't only mean what you show listeners. It also refers to the "word pictures" you create in your listeners' minds—in other words, to *speaking visually*. In addition, you yourself are a strong visual component of your presentations! Your stance, movement, and gestures function as powerful amplifiers of the things you're saying, adding an important visual dimension that colors your words, concepts, ideas, and stories.

Those components of your performance should function that way. If you suffer from speaking anxiety, however, you may have difficulty integrating verbal and physical components in your talks. Strong feelings of self-consciousness, for example, can make you stiffen up and use gestures that are either too tentative or overly formal.

---

3   Brian Stelter, "8 Hours a Day Spent on Screens, Study Finds," *New York Times*, March 27, 2009.

Extreme nervousness can make you stand as still as a statue, as though a chasm surrounds you and one step in the wrong direction means oblivion.

What happens, on the other hand, when you "broadcast confidence" through an easy and practiced use of body language? Here are some positive outcomes:

- You come across as a credible and confident speaker who seems to enjoy what he or she is doing.
- Your voice supports your message with sufficient power and resonance, since vocal production is a physical process.
- You seem more comfortable in your skin.
- Large audiences don't intimidate you.
- You appear to be accessible (not stiff and defensive), which means you're more likable and therefore more persuasive.

That's not a bad set of advantages from simply "looking the part."

This chapter of *Fearless Speaking* is concerned with getting you to be that kind of speaker. It will help make you more poised and confident-looking, someone who obviously enjoys speaking in public. Once you're able to achieve these physical aspects of public speaking, you'll look like you're having a ball, even if speech anxiety is on your dance card!

WHAT IS YOUR BODY SAYING?

So how can you become a dynamic speaker who compels an audience's attention through the physical choices you make?

Clearly, you have to exhibit confidence and a sense of authority. One of the best ways to do so is by a strong stance and the ability to command the space around you. In other words, you must exhibit physical presence. That starts with something really simple: your posture.

Think of it this way: *How you stand affects your* STANDING *with your audience.*

Try this simple exercise:

Stand in front of a mirror. If your posture (your "standing!") needs to improve—if you slouch with shoulders hunched or lean backward putting too much pressure on your lower back—here's a visualization that can help:

IMAGINE THERE'S A STRING LEADING UPWARD

FROM THE TOP OF YOUR HEAD INTO INFINITY.

Someone up there is gently and steadily pulling on that string, causing you to slowly straighten your posture. Gradually, your hips, waist, shoulders, neck, and head each fall into their natural alignment.

Your posture is now straight but not stiff.

Here's an alternate version: Stand with your back against a wall, with your head, backside, and heels all touching the wall. Take a small step forward then relax slightly. Your posture is now improved, though again, not stiff or rigid.

Exercise 4-1, "Grounding" that follows is another visualization that can help improve your posture. This exercise does something much more powerful as well: it brings you closer to the commanding physical presence discussed above. The technique is a fundamental tool of performance that comes to you straight from the world of the actor.

EXERCISE 4-1

GROUNDING

Actors understand that part of their power in performance comes from the earth, or in the modern theater, the stage floor. In the earliest forms of Western theater in ancient Greece, actors performed outside on the ground itself. Visualize a ballet dancer's leap upward and you'll understand where the power for all forms of theatrical performance originates: from the earth under one's feet.

When you ground yourself as a speaker, you acquire the same power and connection to the earth as those ancient tragedians and comedians. The steadfastness and sense of purpose you then display is instantly noticeable to your audience. Consequently, you'll be showing the exact opposite of nerves and self-consciousness.

Here's how to acquire such unwavering physical presence when you speak:

- *Plant your feet firmly on the floor, at armpit width apart. And "plant" is the perfect word! Imagine that you're a 300-year-old oak tree with roots that go deep and wide into the earth. Like that tree, you are firm, secure, and unshakeable. For just a moment, weaken your strong stance by standing with your legs crossed, then leaning on one hip, then standing with your feet touching (like a toy tin soldier). You can easily see how these common stances can weaken an audience's impression of a speaker, since it seems like challenges or harsh questions would blow such a speaker over!*

- *Do you feel when you ground yourself that your self-image strengthens? Doesn't it seem to you like you're suddenly holding your ground?*

Develop a habit of standing this way as soon as you get up in front of others to speak. An interesting thing will happen: *other physical expressions of confidence* will begin to emerge, as a self-regulating cycle of physical strength and confidence will become part of your speaking persona.

I'll share a story with you of the benefit of just a few minutes of grounding for someone who found herself in a highly stressful speaking situation:

A few months ago, I conducted a "Lunch-and-Learn" workshop for the women's networking group of a local Chamber of Commerce. As part of the seminar, I took a volunteer from the audience to demonstrate the importance of breathing, body language, and other aspects of nonverbal communication. The young woman who volunteered was obviously nervous.

She spoke for about five minutes on the topic I suggested: her non-profit organization's mission in the community. I then coached her to overcome her nervousness. I showed her how to slow down and deepen her breathing, and to ground herself, as in the exercise you just completed. She improved at once, as the other women in the group all testified.

A few weeks later, I received a lovely email from the young woman telling me how helpful she had found the exercise to be. She was the maid of honor at her cousin's wedding, and had to speak at the reception. She was very nervous about it, worrying that she wouldn't do a good job and would somehow spoil her cousin's special day. Then, she said, she remembered to ground herself so she was standing strongly, and to breathe diaphragmatically. "Immediately," she wrote, "I calmed down and felt like I was completely present for my toast. It went wonderfully. Thank you for helping me that day at the workshop!"

You can experience exactly the same benefit: Combine the deep-rooted sense of presence you just practiced by "grounding," with the diaphragmatic breathing you learned in Chapter Three of *Fearless Speaking.—Now you'll both look and feel like a person of consequence.* Your self-image itself will help lessen your nervousness.

The following section features another tip along these lines.

HOW TO LOOK MORE CONFIDENT

Try this simple experiment: Stand and expel all the air from your lungs until they're empty. What did that do to your posture? You probably assumed a caved-in appearance, making you look (and feel) weak and lacking in purpose. Now, slowly fill your lungs up to their full capacity.

Did that straighten you up? Do you feel more capable, prepared, *stronger*? I bet you do—and I guarantee that's how your audience will perceive you.

Along with the "Grounding" exercise you just completed, you're combining stance, breathing, and posture in a way that will boost your credibility and authority with audiences. In fact, it's incredible how simple physical techniques like these can alter your stage presence and leadership qualities!

Now you can go one step further to begin controlling *space*. Did you know, for instance, that your use of the physical space around you when you speak could alter an audience's perception of you?

You must therefore avoid the mistake of using space poorly, as some presenters do. Those speakers are too wrapped up in their content and their nervousness to be in control of the performance space around them. If they think about their position on stage or at the front of the room at all, it's only to reflect on how uncomfortable they are standing before *all these people*. And chances are they're also thinking that they don't know what to do with their hands (more about that in a moment).

Speakers who "command space" know how to positively influence their audience's response to them and their message. They realize that the more comfortable they appear to be physically, the more likely audience members will identify with them and be inclined to accept what they say.

Obviously, you need to be that type of speaker.

Dealing with Space. One of the ways that you can invite your listeners' respect and acceptance of what you say is by *occupying an appropriate amount of space*. That means, on the one hand, not diminishing your authority by reducing the amount of space you take up on stage (and thereby apologizing for your presence), and on the other, pacing back and forth like a caged animal (what I call "the motivational speaker syndrome").

You can experiment with your own comfort level regarding how much space you like to occupy as a presenter, but please do incorporate movement into your presentations. This includes when you're behind a lectern. Just because you're using a lectern to hold your notes doesn't mean you can't occasionally step away from this obstacle that's standing between you and your audience.

Here's a good way to get a sense of your own comfort level in terms of using body language: Pay attention to your physical sensations when you're doing something enjoyable, i.e., how you stand, gesture, and use movement and facial expressions. Go back to Exercise 3-1, "Progressive Relaxation" if you need to, to remind yourself of the concept of muscle memory.

Doing so will give you a sense of how you respond physically when you're not self-conscious. Now practice *recreating* those body movements and positions at will. First, allow this to happen before an imaginary audience, then in front of a real one.

You can start right now, in fact, with the following exercise. It's called "Entering a Room."

EXERCISE 4-2

ENTERING A ROOM

If you're still wondering how big a role nonverbal communication plays in public speaking, remember this: an audience starts judging you before you even open your mouth. Once people realize you're the speaker, they'll start watching you and making decisions about you: What's your level of expertise? Are you a likeable person? Are you friendly? Arrogant? Nervous? Inexperienced? The list is endless. These attributes that audiences decide you possess (whether you do or not!) predispose them to accept or reject what you say.

Obviously, if you're aware of your physical expressiveness and consciously use it to your advantage, you'll be helping audiences accept rather than reject you. Such physical expression includes the way you enter a room or walk to the lectern. Even those simple acts can help determine how receptive listeners will be to you. Have you noticed, for instance, how many speakers perform these mundane tasks awkwardly or timidly? They'll "sneak" in, rush forward, march determinedly on with head down, or ignore the audience completely!

In the exercise below, you'll practice something else instead: getting your presentation off to a good start. Your task in this exercise is straightforward: to enter a room (the actual room where you're practicing right now), walk to the point where you'll be speaking, then greet your (imaginary) audience. Use a table, bureau, or the top of your television as your "lectern"—it doesn't matter.

Sound easy? Actually, it is easy. We usually make doing a simple task like entering a room where we're speaking more complicated than it really is because of self-consciousness. Remember what it felt like the last time you had to walk down an aisle or cross a stage when everyone was watching?

Since this exercise is so easy, let's make it a bit more interesting: Enter the room twice, first following SCENARIO A, then SCENARIO B. Have the "notes" that each scenario mentions ready beforehand—use real notes from a recent talk or last week's grocery list; you'll see that they're only there to give you something to look down at. Finally, decide upon a specific imaginary audience before you begin, one that's appropriate for the remarks described below.

• •

SCENARIO A: 1. Enter the room quickly. 2. Proceed to your "lectern" without looking at your audience. 3. Take a long moment to read your notes. 4. Now, look up at the audience for the first time and immediately say: "Hello, everyone. I'm pleased to be with you this morning to discuss an issue of great importance to our organization."

• •

SCENARIO B: 1. Enter the room at a moderate pace while looking at your audience. 2. Proceed to your "lectern." 3. Once you're there, take three seconds more to look directly at your audience, nodding slightly or giving them a professional smile. 4. Then say: "Hello, everyone. I'm pleased to be with you this morning to discuss an issue of great importance to our organization."

• •

Presumably everyone is now listening to you intently. Or are they?

If you were sitting in this audience, which of these speakers would you listen to more closely: the speaker in SCENARIO A or SCENARIO B? Which person showed more professional presence upon entering the room? Which one displayed a friendlier and more accessible demeanor? Which speaker showed more interest in his or her listeners? I'd even venture to guess that Speaker B had a somewhat warmer vocal tone as a consequence of his or her overall approach!

Do you see how broadcasting the right physical attributes can not only boost your self-assuredness and control, but build your credibility, accessibility, and effectiveness with your audience?

WHAT SHOULD I DO WITH MY HANDS?

Now that you're entering your speaking space strongly and demonstrating confidence and concern for your listeners, let's add *gestures* to your repertoire of helpful body language.

Why are gestures important? Because appropriate gestures support your message and inappropriate gestures detract from it. Gestures that are part of your normal physical expressiveness, for instance, make what you're saying seem effortless and natural. But, self-conscious or weak gestures not only work against free and clear expression; they can call attention to your lack of trust in your own material. And planned gestures that you *think* are a good idea (but never are) usually just call attention to themselves.

Gestures are important to speakers for another reason: They're often on that speaker's mind, when the audience usually couldn't care less about them. For example, people who are worried about their public speaking abilities frequently ask me a particular question: "What should I do with my hands?"

The answer is, not much.

Let me explain:

I give that response because people—figuratively but sometimes literally—tie themselves up into knots worrying about how they should stand, move, and gesture when they speak in public. All that self-awareness, just by itself is bound to make anybody move in unnatural ways!

Here, for instance, is an extreme case I once witnessed: A senior business executive was delivering a talk to a group of consultants on a topic about which he was an expert. Instead of standing naturally at the front of this hotel conference room, this gentleman adopted what looked like a begging posture, with his arms and hands locked tightly together at the elbows and his palms extended upward and outward. His stance seemed to be crying out: "*Please* listen to me . . . I really do have something interesting to say!" It was a very odd stance, to say the least, for an influential CEO speaking on his area of expertise.

So we need to ask the question: Why do so many presenters—some of them quite knowledgeable in their field—leave their normal physical expressiveness behind when they speak in front of others? The answer has to do with *context*.

Any of these speakers would normally be perfectly comfortable physically in situations they understand and are familiar, but give them the task of talking to a group of strangers, or on a topic they're not deeply knowledgeable in, and they suddenly become morbidly conscious of everything they do and say. The result is physical expression that is inappropriate and at times just odd, as though they suddenly become a stranger to the body they live in!

Trusting Your Body. The key to overcoming such extreme self-consciousness when you speak is to trust that you'll gesture in the right way at the right moment. If your attention is where it needs to be—on your listeners rather than yourself—your focus will be appropriate as well: on getting your message across to those listeners. If *that's* what you're thinking, instead of what you look like and how you're moving, your gestures will be natural and supportive of what you're saying.

Let's take an example: Think about the last funny or exciting thing you told a group of your friends. As you told the story, you weren't thinking about what you looked like: you just wanted to get the information across as effectively as possible. Why should it be different in your speeches and presentations? If you give yourself over completely to getting your points across, your gestures will be strongly supportive of your content. In a word, the way you hold yourself and move will be *authentic*.

There is no more effective way to accomplish your goals than to be a credible and authentic speaker.

Speaking from the Neutral Position. Try a simple exercise right now: Stand with your arms hanging still at your sides. It may feel awkward at first, but it looks perfectly natural from others' perspective. Now talk about something that sparks your imagination—that really interests you. Don't bring your hands into the action at all—don't make a single gesture—until exactly the right moment for that gesture. In other words, only make that gesture when you *can't not* do it any longer!

Speaking from the "neutral position" like this and gesturing only when it's absolutely necessary to do so is the answer to the question, "What should I do with my hands?" Your gestures will be less frequent and more meaningful, and truly amplify and support what you're saying.

EXERCISE 4-3

SUITING ACTION TO WORD: USING THE RIGHT GESTURES

Hamlet famously said, "Suit the action to the word, the word to the action." It's ideal advice for taking what you've learned in this chapter about natural physical expression, and tying it to gestures that are appropriate and supportive of your content.

To begin this exercise, write a few paragraphs about something important that you'd like to communicate to an audience. Choose a topic that has these two attributes: 1) it's something that you passionately want to get across to your listeners; and 2) it requires your audience to do something in response.

Once you have your text, look it over and familiarize yourself with it. There's no need to memorize it—that's not the value of this exercise.

What you're going to do instead is use THREE GESTURES THAT AMPLIFY what you're saying. To do this, find three places in your mini-talk where an operative word—an image, strongly held point of view, plea for action, dominant emotion, or any other verbal "peak"—embodies a point of critical importance.

Pair each of those operative words or peaks with a strong gesture. You want three important words or phrases, each with its own distinct gesture. Try to use gestures that start from the center of your body and move outward, rather than swinging your arms or hands at the edges of your body.

Now practice your talk in front of a mirror.

What do you think about your performance?

Were your key words and phrases stronger than they'd be without any gestures? Did your movement make the ideas come alive? Did you appear to be a more confident speaker when you moved instead of remaining still? Was the you in the mirror more dynamic?

I bet you were!

Aside from the point about making gestures limited, clean, and strong enough to punch up what you're saying, there really aren't any rules about how you should use gestures in public speaking. When you embody your message emotionally and forget about what you look like, your gestures will support and amplify your meaning.

Here's a suggestion you might also find useful: Create the conditions for the gesture rather than the actual gesture. When you're focused appropriately like this, the gesture will take care of itself and be right.

That's suiting the action to the word.

EXERCISE 4-4

VIDEOTAPING YOUR PERFORMANCE

As this chapter has shown, your stance, body language, and gestures play an important role in demonstrating your proficiency as a speaker. When you're in control and consciously use your physical expressiveness as a presentation tool, your confidence will grow. Confident presenters simply look the part, and so they feel more successful. That's the basic idea behind this chapter's approach to using body language to broadcast confidence.

Now you're ready to put the physical work you've being doing into a unified whole. You've practiced a) entering a room, b) gesturing naturally, and c) suiting your actions to your words. Now it's time to judge how well you're doing these things by videotaping yourself.

Why should you use videotaping? Believe it or not (which I say because most people hate seeing themselves on video), taping yourself is an excellent tool for reducing your negative self-perception. Despite your possible reluctance to see yourself on tape, the truth is that when you watch yourself you realize you're actually pretty good! That's because videotaping shows that your negative assumptions about your abilities are almost always exaggerated.

So if your goal is to have a realistic view of yourself as a speaker—and it should be—there's no substitute for the video camera. Here's how to go about videotaping your presentations for self-evaluation.

First, make a list of the negative characteristics you're sure you'll see on the video you'll be recording. Provide yourself with a range of values for those negative traits, from invisible to extremely obvious. The RATING SCALE on the next page illustrates how you can go about creating such an assessment instrument. Some possible negative traits are provided, and you should write your own in as well. Of course, you can use this actual ratings instrument if you'd like.[4]

---

4   This scale is based on a similar instrument in Stefan G. Hofmann and Michael W. Otto, *Cognitive Behavioral Therapy for Social Anxiety Disorder: Evidence-Based and Disorder-Specific Treatment Techniques* (New York: Routledge, 2008), 184.

VIDEOTAPING RATING SCALE OF NEGATIVE CHARACTERISTICS

	MY RESPONSE IS INVISIBLE	IT'S SLIGHTLY NOTICEABLE	IT'S APPARENT	IT'S EXTREMELY OBVIOUS
sweating	O	O	O	O
heart pounding	O	O	O	O
shallow breathing	O	O	O	O
gasping for air	O	O	O	O
nauseated	O	O	O	O
voice shaking	O	O	O	O
want to run from room	O	O	O	O
mind going blank	O	O	O	O
losing my focus	O	O	O	O
thinking audience doesn't like me	O	O	O	O
avoiding eye contact	O	O	O	O
soft voice	O	O	O	O
trembling voice	O	O	O	O
weak gestures	O	O	O	O
nervous movements	O	O	O	O

lack of organization	O	O	O	O
poor breathing	O	O	O	O
dry mouth	O	O	O	O
flushed appearance	O	O	O	O
"ums," "ahs," and "likes"	O	O	O	O
awkward pauses	O	O	O	O
looked fearful	O	O	O	O
didn't know topic	O	O	O	O
spoke too fast	O	O	O	O
_____	O	O	O	O
_____	O	O	O	O
_____	O	O	O	O
_____	O	O	O	O
_____	O	O	O	O
_____	O	O	O	O

Now give any presentation you like and videotape it. Once you've done so, watch the tape, rating yourself on the scale with each of the characteristics you listed.

Didn't you score lower than you thought you would on any negative characteristic? For instance: how many traits from the left side of the scale were "extremely obvious"? How many were even "apparent"?

Do you see what's happening here? Once you realize that what you think is showing isn't in fact obvious to the audience, you can give yourself permission to stop defining your presentations in fear-related terms.

If you did in fact check off negative characteristics that were apparent on the rating scale, don't be surprised or discouraged. You're reading this book for a reason, after all. You may still have areas you need to work on in terms of exhibiting anxiety, so the solution is simply to work on them!

Take a look again at Exercise 1-5 "Types of Fear Reduction Techniques" in Chapter One. Try to identify from the column on the left the type of response you were exhibiting in the videotaping. Then make a mental note of the matching fear reduction technique shown in the right-hand column. You can then pay particular attention to the chapter in this book that describes that fear reduction technique.

EXERCISE 4-5

CHECKLISTS FOR BODY LANGUAGE AND USE OF SPACE

Your body is not only an extremely important tool of public speaking effectiveness; it's a vital part of your sense of self-confidence. When you "broadcast" a confident speaking style physically, your audience will react to you positively. Here are two checklists you can use to display confidence and add appropriate physical expression to your message:

BODY LANGUAGE: WAS MY BODY LANGUAGE EFFECTIVE?

○ *Did I appear confident yet relaxed?*

○ *Did I use natural movements while avoiding repetitive gestures?*

○ *Did my gestures amplify the points I was making?*

○ *Was my face expressive of my ideas and emotions?*

○ *Did I make direct and ongoing eye contact?*

USE OF SPACE: DID I COMMAND THE SPACE IN WHICH I MOVED?

○ *Did I "own" my space, holding myself and moving with confidence?*

○ *Was my movement fluid rather than abrupt or jerky?*

○ *Did I sit or stand poised without slouching?*

○ *Was I open physically and not closed off in any way?*

○ *Was I animated instead of appearing stiff and wooden?*

In the next chapter, you'll learn how to use another marvelous tool for public speaking effectiveness: the power of focus. It's one more way of achieving the type of "presence" that persuades and inspires audiences.

VASU

As a member of the global marketing team of a medical devices company, Vasu needed to deliver crisp and detailed presentations. He was a polished speaker with a highly analytical and well organized style, though he had a tendency to dive too deeply into detail. But one characteristic worked against him consistently: ineffective body language.

Vasu's movement and gestures were weakening his crisp speaking style. Each time he presented a new point, for instance, he would *back up* a few steps. This gave his audience the impression that he wasn't fully committed to the point he was making! He would also keep one hand in his pocket for long stretches, and "throw" the other hand out to emphasize a point, as if he was literally tossing away his own ideas. Vasu's body language was clearly a weakness in this otherwise smart and articulate presenter.

I told Vasu we needed to quiet down his speaking style so his listeners could focus on what he was saying. I gave him the simple exercise of keeping his hands completely at his sides when he spoke—the "neutral position" mentioned in this chapter. Though he found this difficult to do, it brought his talking points much more into focus. We then gradually added gestures that were purposeful, spare, and amplified the points he was making. Removing his hand from his pocket was another simple yet effective technique that allowed Vasu to gesture with both hands. By the time he finished the program with me, he had learned this secret of effective public speaking: the body, used appropriately, is one of our most dynamic communication tools.

5

STAYING FOCUSED, MINDFUL, AND ON MESSAGE

PRACTICE EXERCISES

5-1 FOCUSED RELAXATION

5-2 EXERCISES FOR MINDFULNESS

5-3 10 WAYS TO STAY FULLY
FOCUSED WHEN SPEAKING

Through the exercises in the previous chapter of *Fearless Speaking*, you took an important step toward becoming a more dynamic and confident speaker: moving out of your head and into your body. This process actually began with the proper breathing habits you learned in Chapter Three, and continued with the body awareness highlighted in Chapter Four.

Now it's time to build on your improved physical presence by becoming more *mentally* present for your listeners.

This probably means taking a different approach than you're used to in giving speeches and presentations. Naturally, you're always literally present when you speak. If you suffer from speech fright, you aren't always mentally and emotionally present. Distracting thoughts and negative emotions can overwhelm your awareness and push everything else out of the picture—including your audience!

This chapter will show you how to stay focused on your true target: your audience and the message you're giving them. You'll do so by learning the concept of MINDFULNESS. In terms of reducing speaking anxiety, mindfulness refers to *the ability to speak to audiences with total awareness of the task and the people at hand.* In a word, you'll be fully "present" for your listeners—which is all any audience really wants from you.

We'll begin this process by bringing you to a state of "focused relaxation."

WHY YOU NEED TO CALM YOUR NERVES

"Easy does it."

"Take it easy."

"Easy as pie."

It's apparent by how common these sayings are that in America we admire people who not only do things expertly, but who make them seem easy.

I believe one of the reasons we feel this way is that when things are going smoothly—when we're hitting on all cylinders—we're functioning at peak efficiency. And that just feels right.

Some people call this level of performance attaining "flow"; or nowadays, being in the "Zone." Whatever name you attach it to it, it's a feeling of effortlessness. It's an intense pleasure that comes from focusing completely on a task at hand rather than the obstacles in your way.

To reduce your speaking fear, it's extremely important that you bring yourself to this state of *natural relaxation.* Once that's accomplished, you can place your focus where it needs to be: on your message and your listeners, rather than on anxiety-related interference that both makes you self-conscious and takes you out of the here-and-now.

There's a catch to achieving such natural relaxation in terms of public speaking, however: You also need a way to do it *quickly.* When preparing to speak, you won't always have the luxury of a half-hour to relax and get yourself in the right frame of mind. The following exercise solves this dilemma. It's designed to help you achieve maximum awareness in a very short period of time. This exercise is called "Focused Relaxation," and it has another terrific advantage: you can do it *if you only have five minutes to spare*. In fact, "Focused Relaxation" might turn out to be the most productive five-minute exercise in your arsenal.

Variations of this exercise have existed for centuries—in everything from Eastern philosophy and yoga to today's mind-body approach to medicine. Many schools of thought have long recognized the benefits of relaxation, improved focus, a state of semi-meditation, and positive biofeedback. Theater troupes, for instance, have used exercises like this for a very long time. That's not a mystery, since any exercise that improves one's focus is ideal for achieving a more successful performance.

Please try the exercise for yourself now.

EXERCISE 5-1

FOCUSED RELAXATION

1. Find a quiet solitary place. Your office, an empty conference room, or your hotel room can all serve the purpose. In a pinch a toilet stall will do, or even your car parked outside the venue where you'll be speaking. Sit comfortably in a well-supported position, feet flat on the floor.

2. Close your eyes.

3. "Listen" to your breath for the first minute. Pay attention to what happens when you breathe in slowly and calmly. Understand with your body rather than your mind how breathing nourishes and sustains you. Feel the breath flow down your throat, filling your lungs then bringing life-giving oxygen to every cell of your body.

4. Now, focus your awareness on a visual image you "see" in your mind. Make it a simple shape in a neutral color without any emotional overtones: a green circle, a yellow square, a blue triangle. Avoid the color red with its associations of passion and blood.

5. See that object in your mind's eye—color and shape—in as close to crystal clarity as you can manage. This usually takes considerable concentration and practice.

6. As you do so, images, thoughts, feelings, and even sounds may rise in your consciousness. Notice them but don't latch onto them; simply let them continue on their way. Bring your focus back to your image. Do nothing; just let your awareness be.

7. Your breathing will slow and deepen. As it does, you'll achieve a calmer and more concentrated state: one of "focused relaxation." Open your eyes and slowly stand. If you feel any lightheadedness, sit down again, for your body may not be used to taking in this level of oxygen. Notice with your mind and your body what this new state feels like. Maintain this level of calm and focus and relaxed steady breathing as you go about your daily tasks.

How did that feel for you? Take a moment now and debrief your own experience: Did you achieve the combination of calmness and focus the exercise aims for? Was it difficult to maintain your focus because of intrusive thoughts? Were you able to "see" a well-defined colored shape? Whatever areas you found difficult in this exercise are the very ones you should practice to get better at.

Now let's analyze why "Focused Relaxation" is helpful for overcoming your speaking anxiety. There are three reasons that I can think of (you may find more):

It slows and deepens your breathing. As we saw in Chapter Three, "vegetative breathing" or breathing for life is usually shallow respiration. To breathe properly for speech, on the other hand, you need to inhale more deeply creating a reservoir of air that will support your voice. And you need to *control* your exhalation, since it is exhaled air activating your vocal cords that creates speech. Your task of imagining a colored object in the "Focused Relaxation" exercise slows your breathing down. It's something of a sleight-of-hand magician's trick: Concentrating on a shape you need to see in your mind's eye, rather than directly on your breathing, allows you to experience a slower calmer inhalation-exhalation cycle.

It exercises your "focus muscle". (Imagine that there is such a component of your brain.) If you suffer from speaking anxiety, one of your hardest tasks is to focus on the task at hand, rather than the unpleasant sensations you're experiencing. Anything that helps improve your mental focus is good. This exercise challenges you to sharpen your focus by giving you the task of seeing both the color *and* shape of an imaginary object. As you probably discovered, that's not easy to do. By accepting the challenge you're getting invaluable practice in learning how to achieve stronger focus.

It teaches you not to listen to harmful self-talk. This may be the most beneficial aspect of "Focused Relaxation." We all experience random thoughts when we're trying to concentrate on something important. The key to succeeding is not to go down either one of two dead-end streets: (a) following the intrusive thought so your concentration is broken; or (b) saying, "I won't pay attention to that thought!" (For instance, try this: for the next ten seconds, *don't* think of an elephant!) If you give in to either temptation you'll be taking your attention away from where it belongs.

The third avenue you can travel down—the helpful one—is simply to notice the intrusive thought but not latch onto it. That's the approach the exercise asked you to take. Imagine how helpful such a skill will be in your speeches and presentations, when you need to focus on your critical message rather than unwelcome or negative thoughts.

The Wall Street Journal said this recently about the value of observation rather than a too-active response to fear: "Observing your critical thoughts without judging them is a more effective way to tame them than pressuring yourself to change or denying their validity."[5]

LIVING IN THE MOMENT

By remaining relaxed yet focused, then, you'll be much more likely to "live in the moment" of your presentations. That's exactly where both you and your audience need you to be. Let's take a look at three more approaches that will help you accomplish that goal.

The first consists of a powerful tool for achieving full focus and presence in everything from everyday activities to high-stakes speaking. It's a concept I referred to earlier: "mindfulness."

MINDFULNESS

Although the term mindfulness is generally associated with modern Buddhist philosophy, according to the *Oxford English Dictionary* the word has been around since 1561 (as "mindfulnesse"), and in its present form since 1817.[6] The concept is simple yet profound: mindfulness means being fully attentive to the here-and-now, i.e., completely present and attuned to your surroundings.

---

5 Melinda Beck, "Conquering Fear," *The Wall Street Journal*, 4 January 2011.

6 *Oxford English Dictionary*, 2nd ed., 2002, as reported at
   http://en.wikipedia.org/wiki/Mindfulness_%28 Buddhism%29, accessed January 8, 2011.

Consider how far this state is from the experience of full-blown speech anxiety! The inner chaos and self-consciousness of stage fright guarantee that you'll be *dis*connected from everything except your intense and unpleasant internal state. When that happens, you aren't living in the present moment at all but in the *future*, when this painful experience of your presentation will be over.

How to Achieve Mindfulness. The key to achieving mindfulness that will keep you attuned to your message and your audience is to make it a daily habit. If you can become more mindful in *everything* you do, you'll make things much easier for yourself in speaking situations where your concentration is most at risk.

Below are five exercises to help you attain mindfulness on a daily basis. Four of them are from Buddhist author and teacher Thich Nhat Hanh's book *The Miracle of Mindfulness*.[7] I've added a fifth exercise of my own. Try one or two of these exercises today and perhaps two others tomorrow.

Remember that like all habits mindfulness takes time to attain. Yet the benefits for both your public speaking career and other areas of your life are undeniable.

---

7   Thich Nhat Hanh, *The Miracle of Mindfulness: A Manual on Meditation* (Boston: Beacon Press, 1987, revised), 79–90.

EXERCISE 5-2

EXERCISES FOR MINDFULNESS
(From Thich Nhat Hanh, The Miracle of Mindfulness)

THE HALF-SMILE

Just as moods and feelings make us act in specific ways, by assuming a physical pose or expression we can create a particular feeling. "Wearing a smile" is definitely one way we can accomplish this goal.

The Half-Smile: Take hold of your breath. Inhale and exhale three breaths gently while maintaining a half-smile. Follow your breath. Anywhere you find yourself, put on a half-smile. Inhale and exhale quietly three times. Maintain the half-smile and consider the spot of your attention as your own true nature.

MAKE TEA

Mindfulness While Making Tea: *Prepare a pot of tea to serve a guest or to drink by yourself. Do each movement slowly, in mindfulness. Do not let one detail of your movements go by without being mindful of it. Know that your hand lifts the pot by its handle. Know that you are pouring the fragrant warm tea into the cup. Follow each step in mindfulness. Breathe gently and more deeply than usual. Take hold of your breath if your mind strays.*

WASH THE DISHES

Washing the Dishes: *Wash the dishes relaxingly, as though each bowl is an object of contemplation. Consider each bowl as sacred. Follow your breath to prevent your mind from straying. Do not try to hurry to get the job over with. Consider washing the dishes the most important thing in life. Washing the dishes is meditation. If you cannot wash the dishes in mindfulness, neither can you meditate while sitting in silence.*

SLOW-MOTION BATH

A Slow-Motion Bath: *Allow yourself 30 to 45 minutes to take a bath. Don't hurry for even one second. From the moment you prepare the bathwater to the moment you put on clean clothes, let every motion be light and slow. Be attentive of every movement. Place your attention on every part of your body, without discrimination or fear. Be mindful of each stream of water on your body. By the time you've finished, your mind should feel as peaceful and light as your body. Follow your breath. Think of yourself as being in a clean and fragrant lotus pond in the summer.*

TAKE A WALK (GENARD)

Take a walk in the early morning or evening. Do not think of personal matters or business concerns. Instead, focus on your breathing and being outside in the fresh air. An entire world is passing slowly by as you walk. Notice it. Calmly contemplate the things around you of the earth and the air. If there is water nearby, watch and listen to it. Try to do this every day for at least a half-hour.

Let's relate all of the above to a practical application concerning public speaking. The following exercise is a "cheat sheet" you can use while delivering a speech. It offers ten ways to stay focused during your presentation. It's a hands-on way of applying the principles of mindfulness and focus to develop greater confidence and presence.

EXERCISE 5-3

10 WAYS TO STAY FULLY FOCUSED WHEN SPEAKING

1. **Ground yourself.** *Feel your feet gripping the floor. Imagine your feet have roots that go deep into the earth. The earth gives you energy and stability. You are steadfast and powerful!*

2. **Stand or sit with good posture.** *Visually it matters to your audience's perception of you. Overall, it makes a difference in how strongly you and your ideas are accepted. You will feel like you have more authority if you look like you should.*

3. **Breathe.** *Slowly, deeply, calmly. Be aware of each delicious nourishing breath.*

4. **Dive into your audience.** *Your audience is a pool. Submerge yourself in their energy and humanity. Relish the sheer reality of their presence and yours, together.*

5. **Take your time.** *You probably speak too rapidly in fearful situations because adrenaline speeds everything up. Take your time to cherish this speaking opportunity, which will only ever be here now.*

6. **Pay attention with all of your senses.** *Sensually take in everything that's going on around you. Hear with your eyes, feel the audience's reactions as if it were tactile, taste the ideas in your mouth, etc. Respond with all your being!*

7. **Aim your energy outward.** *Your AUDIENCE matters, not you! Lose yourself in your message and how it is being received.*

8. **Make eye contact as you tell the story.** *That's what your audience is here for. Whatever you're talking about, it's a story, a narrative. Tell people about it.*

9. **Trust silence.** *Silence helps you pace your presentation appropriately. Remember, silence can be powerful. It also tells audiences, "I am confident."*

10. **Move!** *If you move while you speak, it will help you think and keep you in the moment. If you're seated, simply use your arms, hands, upper body, and face.*

DEVELOPING MENTAL TOUGHNESS

Let's make the move now from mindfulness and staying focused to another essential attribute of speaking in public: mental toughness.

Are the two divorced in effective speaking? I don't think so. To be "there" for listeners, you need to be fully present in mind and body. To influence people's behavior and lead them to action, you also need the strength that comes from discipline and a rigorous dedication to your goals.

Discipline may seem like a harsh word, but it's a hallmark of craftsmanship and excellence across many fields of endeavor. You can reduce your fear of public speaking without being disciplined, but it will take much longer and the results will be uncertain. Being disciplined will keep you on a straight path that leads directly to your goal. Here are two ways to get there:

1. *Unlearn Multitasking*—Multitasking is the enemy of impactful public speaking. By its nature, multitasking splits your consciousness into partial attention to any task. Remember, an important symptom of speech fright is loss of control: the feeling that you're at the mercy of frightening forces in a moment of crisis. Trying to do more than one thing at a time *reduces* your control over any one of them, and that means reducing your effectiveness as well. Just as with mindfulness, try to develop the habit of concentrating fully on one thing at a time. If you do so in your everyday activities, it will be that much easier when you're giving an important presentation.

2. *Limit Your Speaking Objective*—Presentations are finite events. So, be realistic about what you can reasonably accomplish in 20 minutes, a half-hour, or even in a 90-minute talk. Some people run into problems in this area because they try to bring the entire relationship between themselves and the audience into the action. They might drag in some past history between members of both their organizations, or all of the objections that could possibly be raised about this issue, or the personality conflicts in the room. Imagine trying to deal with all of that while delivering a challenging talk on a specific topic! In my work with clients who have this difficulty, I get them to focus on

the *single purpose* they're trying to accomplish. That's enough of an assignment for a brief presentation.

If you too can limit your objective to something you can accomplish while the window of your presentation is open, you'll be demonstrating mental toughness. From there, it's only a small step to knowing that you can handle yourself *whatever* situation arises. You'll have developed the discipline of focusing on a single task—an admirably realistic gauge of success. For more about defining your objective, go back to Chapter Two and review.

HOW TO POSITIVELY IMPACT YOUR AUDIENCE

So where are you now in terms of staying focused and mindful when you speak?

If you've practiced the exercises in this chapter and continue to do so, you should improve your focus and mindfulness dramatically. You'll turn down the "noise" of your public speaking anxiety and place yourself where you need to be: in the present moment, speaking to audiences that have a genuine interest in what you're saying. Knowing that you have that ability should by itself increase your confidence.

From such a well-focused starting point, you'll be much better positioned to connect with listeners and to achieve the influence you're looking for. Methods of doing so powerfully and memorably are featured in the next chapter.

NADIA

Nadia is the CEO of a service organization representing manufacturers of kitchen and bathroom fixtures. She speaks to groups frequently at conferences and industry-wide meetings. She has situational anxiety, i.e., she's comfortable in front of small groups but is intimidated by large audiences. Since she often speaks to hundreds of people at industry events, she wanted help with the anxiety that had become a constant in her life.

Nadia is a dynamic administrator, and has led her organization to a five-fold increase in revenue in as many years—a remarkable achievement. But somehow none of it mattered when she stood in front of those hundreds of industry insiders.

Her biggest problem was staying on message. She was convinced that she didn't sound credible, and so she would listen to her own negative self-talk. Sometimes this even made her forget her talking points! She would then begin speaking rapidly in a futile effort to get her confidence and rhythm back.

Nadia lacked presence because she literally wasn't present with her audiences, spending all her performance time listening to her own disruptive thoughts. She brought a negative self-image on stage that made it impossible for her to feel or appear confident. I worked with her on each of the "10 Ways to Stay Fully Focused when Speaking" featured in this chapter. The result was remarkable: Nadia was able to settle in to her talks and sound like herself for the first time. Listeners could now see and hear the true Nadia. Here was the dynamic head of her service organization appearing in public at last!

6

HOW TO CONNECT WITH AUDIENCES AND GAIN INFLUENCE

PRACTICE EXERCISES

6-1 GREETING YOUR AUDIENCE

6-2 USING A GRABBER

6-3 CREATING A CLINCHER

This chapter discusses how to get an audience on your wavelength and *make something happen in the room.* It's about opening your presentations strongly, ending memorably, and nailing everything in between. It will show you how to grab your audience and never let go. And it will tell you how to have fun while doing it.

For these great things to happen, you'll have to start from the right place. That means not making your listeners into a collection of Frankenstein monsters. You may not have been thinking of them as seven feet tall with a bolt through their necks, but if you routinely believe that audiences are programmed to respond negatively to you, that's what you've been doing.

Too many speakers are guilty of this—of conjuring up an imaginary audience that's much scarier than the real one. A recent experiment, for instance, found that people with social anxiety pay more attention to negative faces than positive ones.[8] Anxious speakers can *really* put that concept to work, sometimes manufacturing an entire hostile audience out of a few unfriendly faces![9]

What this chapter suggests instead is that you make your default setting a *friendly* group of people who are actually interested in what you're going to say. Then practice *keeping* them interested. Your presentation will be far more engaging. Even more important, you'll be memorable, and you'll have a much greater chance at creating a lasting influence with your audience.

Let's look at four specific ways you can create such a positive impact on listeners.

> *A recent experiment, for instance, found that people with social anxiety pay more attention to negative faces than positive ones.*

4 KEY METHODS OF ACHIEVING INFLUENCE AS A SPEAKER

We give speeches, presentations, sales talks, pitches, keynotes, and every other type of oral performance to *influence* listeners. Audiences know this—it's the reason they're in the room: to get information or insight that will make their lives easier or more fulfilling. So rather than resisting you, most audience members are on your side and want you to succeed—for their sake as well as your own. Here are four actions you can take to help yourself succeed and connect with your audiences. You should include these in every one of your presentations.

---

8   Hofmann and Otto, *Cognitive Behavioral Therapy for Social Anxiety Disorder*, 16, citing a study by L.-G. Lundh and L.-G. Öst, "Recognition bias for critical faces in social phobics," in *Behaviour Research and Therapy*, 34, 787-794 (1996). In the study, subjects with social anxiety disorder or SAD and controls were asked to judge from photographs whether people were critical or accepting in nature. After performing an unrelated task, both groups were given a facial recognition test. People with social anxiety disorder more easily recognized the people they thought had critical faces, while the control subjects had a tendency to recall "accepting" faces.

9   If in fact there are any unfriendly faces. Many audience members simply have features that have set in certain ways that have nothing to do with whether they're friendly or unfriendly by nature.

1. **Establish Your Credibility.** To get listeners to think, feel, or do what you want them to as a result of your speech, you must have *credibility*. "Why in the world should I listen to this person?" is the question every listener wants the answer to. It's up to you to supply the answer. And *fast*: during the first 60 seconds or so of your talk.

   Tell them why they should listen to you—and I mean literally tell them. What's your level of experience to speak on this topic? One way you can supply the right answer to that question is to give your job title when you introduce yourself.[10] Mention the number of years you've been working in this field. If this topic has been a hobby or avocation of yours for 20 or 30 years, tell them! If you did any research with regard to this talk, tell them that too. You need to establish your *bona fides*, since being a credible speaker is what kick-starts your audience into paying attention, and eventually into believing what you say.

2. **Be Honest.** Sound obvious? Actually, when you lack confidence in yourself as a presenter, you start down a path toward dishonesty with your audience. Such dishonesty can manifest itself as trying to be something different from what you really are (often, for instance, aiming to be more like a speaker you admire instead of being true to yourself). Or it can show itself as defensiveness or retreating into a self-protective mode. When you take one of these approaches, it changes the way you hold yourself, move, sound, and relate to strangers. Audiences sense such dishonesty immediately and turn off their "trust switch."

   The good news here is that you are absolutely unique—and therefore interesting in your own right. You'd be a pretty poor Bill Clinton or Oprah Winfrey . . . but they'd also make a pretty miserable *you*. To get listeners to trust you and respond positively to your message, give them the real you with all of your vulnerabilities. That's the person they came to hear.

---

10 And please, give the audience your full name. "Hi, I'm Brenda!" isn't going to do much to establish strong credibility.

3. **Think Like Your Audience.** Never forget that when you speak you're there for the audience's benefit not your own. Therefore, you need to find ways to put yourself in their shoes so you can understand and meet their needs.

    If possible, greet some of your audience members before your presentation. Shake hands. Become acquainted in some small way so these people aren't strangers when you get up to speak. And please, make eye contact. Some presenters are so nervous that they look over the heads of the audience. But as I say to my clients who confess to doing this: Who's easier to convince, your listeners or the back wall?

    Equally important: watch your listeners' reactions since you may need to adjust your approach. If you've been speaking in generalities and notice that people are getting fidgety, bring in a story that illustrates your point. If they're having trouble grasping a connection, use a comparison from their world so they'll understand. If people are looking confused, ask if everyone is still with you—people may tell you where you lost them. By employing any or all of these techniques, you'll ensure that they'll stay connected to you minute-by-minute.

4. **Lead Them to *Action*.** Too many speakers simply throw information at listeners. Instead of doing that, you be the speaker who builds in actionable content. Think beforehand about what you want your audience to *do* as a result of your presentation. Ask yourself what you'd like them to take away—or better yet, the action you want them to take.

    One way to think of this is to ask: *"Exactly how do I plan to change people's lives as a result of my speech?"* Now you'll be talking!

    When you think in terms of action, you give your presentation drive, a sense of movement, and relevance. You'll be drilling down to why your speech really matters. Understand that, and you'll immediately gain a huge boost in confidence.

Clearly, then, successful speaking means being honest and caring about your audience more than it has to do with being an "excellent" speaker. Revealing your true self to a group of strangers may be anxiety provoking for you, but, in the end, it means that you'll have a genuine dialogue with listeners rather than faking it.

Trying to hide from an audience is the *really* difficult thing, because it's almost impossible to pull off. Sharing your knowledge with listeners, on the other hand, is easy. Let's look at how combining honesty with openness will help you connect even more strongly with audiences.

SHOW AUDIENCES YOUR GOOD WILL

Audiences need to feel that you're speaking for their benefit. Yet, how many speakers convey the opposite impression: some who seem more concerned with their speaking fee than their listeners; those who are most concerned with selling their products in the back of the room; and the bores who love the sound of their own voices. You can find them right now, in your city or anywhere around the world.

"Good will," on the other hand, which means being more concerned with an audience's profit than your own, is one of the things that will change you from being an ordinary speaker into a valuable one. You can educate yourself about establishing and maintaining good will in public speaking. The next time you're in a meeting or attending a presentation, ask yourself what the speaker's main concern seems to be: Is it sharing an important message with listeners or looking good in the spotlight?

Here are some clues to look for:

Is the speaker's eye contact strong? Does he or she pay attention to the audience's nonverbal communication indicating engagement or restlessness? Is this presenter's "soliloquy" put on pause occasionally to solicit input from the audience?

Think about that skill of eye contact for a moment—such an important indicator of a speaker's connection with an audience. How can anyone be truly concerned with the needs of their listeners, for instance, if the PowerPoint screen at the front of the room is more important to them than the people listening? Eye contact is just one of the indications (though it's a key one) of whether a speaker is on a two-way avenue of presenter-audience interaction, or heading down a dead-end street.

The lesson is inescapable: Confident speakers place their listeners front-and-center at all times. They look at people and use facial expressions freely—exactly the way you do when you're talking with friends.

You may think it's difficult to look at audience members if you have speaking anxiety. But that's the very reason it's essential to do so: when you pay attention to other people's responses, you can't excessively monitor your own. *Voila!* You've become a speaker who obviously cares more about the audience than about himself.

There's no better way to demonstrate your good will toward your listeners.

STAYING TRUE TO YOURSELF

Now let's talk about staying true to yourself as a speaker. This may seem difficult at first if you have speaking anxiety, but it's actually a necessary and rewarding aspect of your speech performances.

One of the fascinating things about speaking in public is that it reveals so much about who you are as a human being. As I tell clients: even as an actor, I would have to work ferociously hard to hide my true nature when I talk to audiences about something that really matters to me. And if I did that, all of my energy would be directed *inward* instead of where it needs to be—on keeping my audience actively engaged with my critical message. It's exactly the same in your speeches and presentations.

Public speaking situations only become uncomfortable when you perceive them as something different from everyday conversation— which in fact they're not as I'll explain in a few paragraphs. When you think of presentations with a capital "P" and speeches with a capital "S", they become formal and intimidating. That's when you get nervous and afraid. You're no longer on the wavelength of simply *talking* to people as you do in everyday conversations. To protect yourself in these now "dangerous" situations, you slip on a presentation mask or don invisible protective armor.

So, you become someone you're not and audiences sense it immediately. The simple but powerful solution is to throw away the mask, to let your true self come through. You need to do this for your listeners, of course, but also for yourself.

How can you stay true to yourself? One of the simplest and most effective ways is to remember that you're having a conversation with your listeners in which influence is *exchanged*. You don't have to be an actor to understand that having a dialogue with someone is much easier than delivering a monologue!

HAVE A DIALOGUE WITH YOUR LISTENERS

If you're thinking by now that lots of speeches and presentations are more of a *monologue* than a dialogue, you're right. Too many people approach presentations with the idea that they're one-way conversations in which the speaker gives out information and the audience receives it passively. Bad presentations can certainly give that impression, since there's no give-and-take going on. It's no wonder that speakers who find themselves in those situations feel isolated and exposed in front of audiences.

Good presentations, on the other hand, have an entirely different feel about them. And when you're giving one of those talks, you know it and so does your audience.

That's because when you're delivering a dynamic talk, information passes back and forth continuously. It's true that most information is verbal on your part and nonverbal on the part of your audience (except in Q & A). Yet that's a critically important exchange!

Think about it: Isn't your audience passing you information *every second*? It's in the form of eye contact, head nods, smiles, laughter, etc.—in other words, it is in nonverbal communication. And that means that every one of your presentations actually *is* more of a dialogue than a monologue, doesn't it?

The lesson for you here is to *pay attention to that nonverbal communication coming your way*. That's your audience's "speech" in the moments when they aren't actually asking questions or challenging something you said.

Do this and you'll truly be more conversational with your listeners. You'll be fully present, for one thing, and your audience will sense much more of a connection with you. And it really is amazing how people are more persuaded by someone talking *to* them rather than at them.

Ready to take this concept for a test drive? Exercise 6-1, "Greeting Your Audience" that follows is an ideal way to practice getting off to a solid start with listeners, as described above.

EXERCISE 6-1

GREETING YOUR AUDIENCE

The greeting of your speech or presentation is critically important. Too few speakers understand this, but you need to. Otherwise, you short-change your audience by ignoring what's going on in these first few moments of your talk, which boils down to not connecting or establishing rapport with them.

Your greeting precedes your introduction, which means it's actually the first thing you say to your listeners. So you need to get it right, for these reasons:

1. The audience is anticipating what's coming as "the curtain rises."

2. Listeners are paying maximum attention at this point.

3. You say something directly to the audience before getting into the topic.

4. The tone is set for everything that follows.

5. Your audience experiences you at your most unguarded and honest.

6. Everyone is reminded that they're about to share something.

7. People are exposed to your personality before information gets in the way.

Unsure about that last point? After all, aren't you there to convey information? Yet information never influences people as much as you do. You simply use information to succeed at doing so. Another way to think of this is, however valuable your information is, it is only there to help you accomplish your purpose with this audience.

Too many speakers, however, toss away the golden moment of the greeting. They broadcast their nervousness, pay more attention to their notes than the people in front of them, or spend their first few minutes talking to the projection screen!

Your job instead is to establish rapport with your audience and show them you're going to be interesting.

How do you do that? Simple: give your listeners—not your notes and not your nervousness—all of your focus. You can practice this right now:

1. *Compose a short greeting for an imaginary presentation. If you have one coming up that you'd like to prepare for, that's even better. You can start with "hello" or "good morning," or by thanking someone who just introduced you. Once you've written this out, look it over then turn the page face down.*

2. *Smile. Now deliver your greeting without looking away from your audience for even a second. If you forgot something you wrote down, no problem—stop, look over what you've written then start again. But don't look down at your notes while you're talking. MAKE THE AUDIENCE THE ENTIRE FOCUS OF YOUR GREETING.*

It's important to do this, because audiences need to trust you and find you a credible speaker if they are going to open up to you and allow you to change their minds and their actions.

If, however, like many nervous speakers you disrespect your audience by giving them only partial attention, they'll find it difficult to warm up to you. Use your own response as a guide: do you trust people who don't look you in the eye when they're talking to you? If you start out from such a weak position as a speaker, you'll have a hard time persuading and moving audiences.

Let's move on now from your greeting to the substance of your presentation. You've greeted your audience strongly. Now it's time to capture their full attention and engagement concerning your topic. You do so by coming up with an irresistible *grabber*.

HOW TO GRAB AN AUDIENCE

We'll start by discussing two important concepts concerning how an audience pays attentions and retains what you say: *primacy* and *recency*. "Primacy" states that audiences remember best what you say to them initially. "Recency" makes a similar claim for what you said most recently. In terms of presentations, these terms translate into your Introduction and Conclusion.

Your Introduction. There are at least three reasons why your Introduction needs to be engaging and interesting *immediately*:

(1) Audiences make value judgments about you and your message in the first 30-60 seconds. After this point, you'll be able to alter those opinions about as easily as you can change concrete back into cement and water.

(2) Your opening sets the tone for your entire presentation.

(3) This is when you introduce your message and tell the audience why they should listen.

In other words, your introduction is the moment when your audience starts viewing you in a positive light. Of course, it's also the time when you're most nervous and self-conscious. The solution to both challenges—gaining a favorable impression from your audience and putting yourself at ease—is an effective grabber.

A Grabber's Task. A good grabber *intrigues* your audience concerning what they're about to hear. If it also surprises them a little, so much the better. These responses—intrigue, surprise, and engagement— won't happen if you start out with the uninteresting "Today-I'm-going-to-talk-about-dot-dot-dot" approach: in other words, simply (and blandly) announcing your topic.

Why not *captivate* your listeners instead? Below are some tried-and-true methods for engaging your audience immediately—what I call "grabbers." They're rhetorical devices that speakers have been using to good effect for millennia.

Feel free to use one of these or come up with your own hook. The list isn't exhaustive by any means. Only two things limit effective grabbers: appropriateness to the topic and audience at hand, and your imagination.

So, once you've greeted your audience and established a feeling of rapport and interest in them, give them a grabber.

EFFECTIVE GRABBERS

- Question (rhetorical or otherwise)
- Story
- Statistic
- Catchy fact
- Startling statement
- Intriguing challenge you pose for the audience
- Quotation
- Expert testimony
- Personal anecdote
- Client testimonial or endorsement
- Scientific data
- Reports, case studies, findings, etc.
- Visual
- Humor
- Activity
- Demonstration
- Today's headline or top news story
- Sound cue or music
- Company or industry hot item
- "Imagine . . ." (a scenario that you'll then build on or refute)[11]

---

11 You probably noticed that this list doesn't include video clips. I don't recommend that you *start out* with one. Your credibility and influence with an audience depend upon your being the leader in the room, especially at the opening of your talk. Videos instantly steal the spotlight and become the primary influencer for that part of your presentation—at precisely the moment when you need to establish such authority yourself.

Want an example?

Here's a grabber I used recently. An interesting aspect of this opening is that I didn't know I was going to use it until the words were coming out of my mouth! If that happens, your grabber won't be any less effective (and might be more effective) because of it. That's because your subconscious may give you what you need at exactly the right moment, when you aren't even thinking about it. Such grabbers can be particularly appropriate because they spring organically from the moment at hand.

That's what happened to me.

The Scene:

It's 10:00 a.m. on the first morning of a two-day training I'm conducting at the United Nations on "Effective Speaking for Diplomats." This is the second time in consecutive years that I'm conducting this seminar on behalf of the United Nations Institute for Training and Research (UNITAR). We're gathered in one of the conference rooms in the General Assembly building, where diplomatic staff from 18 countries is present. It's time to begin, and a representative from UNITAR has just introduced me.

The Grabber:

I thank the introducer; give my name and what I do. Then I hear myself saying:

"Ladies and gentlemen: you know you're at the United Nations when you visit the rest room, and the graffiti[12] on the wall says: 'Fair trade now!' Of course, graffiti in men's rooms is usually of an entirely different nature—but that's what I saw just now down the hall. And it reminded me what a pleasure it is to be back at the United Nations, working with some of the world's best speakers, on some of the most important topics in the world. Today and tomorrow, we'll be . . . ."

---

12 I know that's grammatically incorrect, but somehow, "The graffito on the wall" doesn't sound quite right!

And I was off and running.

My grabber's gentle humor elicited chuckles rather than guffaws, which was just what I was looking for. Using humor instead of a far riskier joke means that your grabber probably won't be earth shattering, but it doesn't need to be. A grabber should engage your listeners, invite their attentiveness, get you off to a springboard start, and help you move organically into your topic. Not bad for the first 20 to 30 seconds of your presentation!

Compare my humorous opening, for instance, with the typical "I'm-going-to-talk-about-dot-dot-dot" approach, which in my case would have been:

"Today, we're going to look at how diplomats can speak more effectively."

Ho-hum, right?

Now it's your turn to use this essential device of speeches and presentations in Exercise 6-2 below.

EXERCISE 6-2

USING A GRABBER

Your grabber needn't be wildly creative and you shouldn't agonize over it. It does however require some thought, a little imagination, and a pinch of creativity. The idea behind an effective grabber is that you know your topic—and so you understand how to get your audience interested in it. You shouldn't need more than 15 to 30 minutes to come up with an opening that will launch your talk successfully. The alternative, as we've seen above, is to opt for a standard (spelled B-O-R-I-N-G) opening.

So here you go:

STEP ONE: Find a presentation you've done previously and familiarize yourself with it again.

STEP TWO: Think about your audience and what your purpose was in giving this presentation. Those two factors—audience and purpose—are the most important aspects of creating your grabber. As you get ready to introduce your listeners to your topic, ask yourself these questions: What interests these people? What turns them on and "touches them where they live"? Knowing the answer to these questions, ask yourself what type of approach will draw them into your topic and message immediately. Would relating a PERSONAL EXPERIENCE do it? A HANDS-ON ACTIVITY? A remark concerning something in their INDUSTRY? What about a reference to POPULAR CULTURE?

STEP THREE: Now refer to the "Effective Grabbers" list above. Which of those rhetorical devices will allow you to gain impact and involvement immediately?

STEP FOUR: Decide on a grabber and spend a little time shaping it. Practice it a couple of times in a simulated "launch" of your presentation. (Which grabber did you choose?)

STEP FIVE: Try it a few more times until you can do it smoothly. Videotape yourself and watch the results.

What do you think? I'll bet you came up with something far more interesting than just blandly announcing your topic. If the grabber you just created is a more dynamic opening than what you did in your original presentation, so be it. Think about using it or something similar next time!

BRAVO! – ENDING DRAMATICALLY AND MEMORABLY

Once you've delivered the body of your presentation, you're ready for your finale. And here you have a specific task: to make your ending *memorable*. Just as a sumptuous dinner begs for a delectable dessert, a strong presentation needs a powerful conclusion. It will ensure that your influence continues once you stop talking. You may have just delivered fabulous information—but what good is it if your audience forgets it the moment they step out into the corridor?

Earlier in this chapter, you were introduced to the concept of primacy: the theory that audiences will strongly retain what they experience first. Now we can discuss *recency*, which states that listeners are likely to recall the last thing you say.

"Quit while you're ahead," and "Always leave 'em laughing," are two well-known sayings that embody the principle of recency.

To understand the vital importance of a strong conclusion, ask yourself this question: Out of all the speeches and presentations you've listened to in the past year, how many of them ended memorably? How many of them even *had* a well thought-out conclusion?

One of the most common speech shortcomings, then, is the lack of a memorable ending that can drive the speaker's message home. An audience may be forced to sit through a shaggy dog finish to a speech that goes on and on, or they may arrive at a cliff over which the presentation abruptly plummets as soon as the last point is made. In these cases and others, audience members may reasonably ask: "Where's the *ending*?" A speech without a conclusion leaves listeners hungry for that last satisfying bite of dessert.

Why do this to an audience that has stayed engaged with your presentation up to now?

Get in the habit instead of delivering a finish that's every bit as memorable as the key points of your talk. Or even more so! Your ending has to "close the deal," by getting your listeners to buy into the way of thinking, feeling, or acting you've been advocating.

I call concluding like this using a *clincher*.

Just as with your grabber, a solid clincher takes a bit of thought and a dash of creativity. Over the centuries, knowledgeable speakers have developed certain rhetorical devices to help them conclude strongly. Can you guess where such devices are to be found? If you're thinking, "In the same list that included grabbers," you're right! A question or quotation, memorable story or personal anecdote, or any of the other approaches listed above as grabbers will help you conclude your speech with maximum style and substance.[13]

Make Your Clincher "Sticky". Speakers sometimes use a clincher that refers back to their grabber. For instance, if you spoke about someone's personal experience to open your talk, you may end with the conclusion of that story. (And speakers have been known to hold an audience in suspense concerning how someone's story turned out!) An approach like that ties an opening and closing together and can have a satisfying symmetry. But it's not necessary to use that method. It is necessary to be sufficiently dramatic, provocative, or intriguing that your message will stick in the listener's mind afterwards.

That in fact is a good way to think of an effective clincher: it's *sticky*.

---

13 And don't forget: you can come up with a clincher of your *own* invention!

EXERCISE 6-3

CREATING A CLINCHER

Have some fun and try something right now: Take the presentation you chose for the grabber (Exercise 6-2 above), and create a clincher for that same talk. Remember to keep your purpose and your audience in mind, and remind yourself of the grabber you came up with. Try one or more clinchers on for size, see which you like the fit of, and videotape yourself delivering it a couple of times.

Now step back and admire your handiwork: Do you have a more interesting opening and closing to this presentation than you had originally? If the answer is yes, you now have a proven method for succeeding at what this chapter set out to help you do: make a lasting impression on your audiences.

Well done! You now possess a trio of powerful tools—your greeting, grabber, and clincher—for connecting with listeners and improving their perception of you as a speaker. From the first moment of your speech to the last, you've strengthened your ability to energize, engage, and entertain audiences. You're now a big step closer to more confident and successful performances in public.

SANTIAGO

Sometimes a client who is looking for speech training understands exactly how he or she needs to improve. In other cases, this person may be focused on certain problem areas but miss others of greater importance. Santiago fell into the second category.

A sales manager for a financial services company, Santiago was in a client-facing role and frequently had to speak at client meetings. He was extremely self-conscious and nervous in these situations. He didn't suffer anticipatory anxiety, but while talking he was convinced people were judging him, and so rushed to get his presentations over with as quickly as possible. "I don't prepare a lot, or I prepare at the last minute," he told me. Then he added: "The point is I know my material backwards and forwards."

That last comment was the key to Santiago's problem. He *did* know his material thoroughly, but he was ignoring his need to prepare. Mark Twain once said, "I didn't have time to write a short letter, so I wrote a long one instead." Presentations are windows of opportunity that close quickly. To make everyone's time worthwhile, they need to be both carefully thought out and concisely delivered.

Santiago's feeling that he was being negatively judged probably stemmed from the fact that his talks weren't well organized. He did a good job setting out his main points, but his transitions were weak and his conclusions nonexistent. Audiences had a hard time following his argument logically, and he always ended abruptly. We worked specifically on taking the time to *engage* his listeners' attention, beginning and ending memorably (with a grabber and clincher), and using logical transitions. His talks became as organized as they were knowledgeable, and his nervousness while presenting disappeared.

7

UNLEASH YOUR VOCAL POWER!

The 2010 film "The King's Speech" about stammering King George VI of England taught audiences about the power of one's personal voice. Each of us—whether we're a sales rep, little league coach, or President of the United States—needs to have faith in our own voice. The truth is that it's not only what we say but also the unique way we say it that gives legitimacy to our presentations. And the good news is that we all possess an inborn talent to speak with originality and effectiveness.

Faith in your voice, then, can give you tremendous confidence as a speaker. Your voice is exceptional because it is yours alone. No one—not the King of England himself!—can speak in your voice and give audiences what they came to hear.

This chapter of *Fearless Speaking* will help you give free and full expression to your vocal uniqueness, which is a powerful tool for increasing your self-confidence. You see, when you believe in your own voice, you cannot be silenced—not even by your own fears and perceived inadequacies in other areas.

Bear in mind, however, that you will never be a perfect speaker. Such a creature doesn't exist! You'll actually be something much more interesting: a presenter who goes beyond the mere delivery of information to express who you are fundamentally as a person. And, in the end, that's what audiences are looking for: a real person. When you can *get out of your own way* as a speaker, everything you have to offer will come through clearly and powerfully. This chapter will help you find ways to make that happen in terms of your vocal skills.

> *You see, when you believe in your own voice, you cannot be silenced—not even by your own fears.*

ARE YOU SINGING YOUR SPEECH OR JUST MOUTHING THE WORDS?

Did you ever consider that delivering an outstanding presentation is like performing a great song? Not only is the "music" delightful to listen to, but also your voice soars on a combination of dynamic technique and an inspirational message. The way you use your vocal tools, for instance your vocal tone, pitch, and/or emphasis, carries astonishing weight in helping you to establish credibility, authority, and that all-important attribute, believability.

Why does your voice make such a difference? Well, for one thing, we all respond in basic and even primitive ways to the qualities of a person's voice. If a voice is pleasant and authoritative, for instance, it inspires confidence in the listener. But a voice that comes across as unpleasant, weak, or too timid nudges that same listener in the opposite direction.

Vocal dynamics, or vocal variety, is one of the most effective tools you own for winning over audiences in that positive direction. The elements of vocal dynamics—tone quality, pitch placement, inflection, use of emphasis, variations in pace and tempo, pauses, and all the emotional nuances your voice can project—provide a nearly limitless palette to "paint word pictures" and convince others. When you employ good vocal dynamics, you make your stories and ideas come vibrantly alive for your listeners.

The potential of your voice. One effective way to realize your vocal potential is to keep in mind that the voice is inherently physical. That fact may sound obvious, but it's easy to forget when you're preoccupied with the content of a presentation or consumed by performance anxiety.

Because your voice is physical, it is intimately connected to energy and relaxation, as well as tension and stress. That means that the pressures of a too-hectic lifestyle or work schedule will emerge in one form or another in your vocal expression. Anything you can do to relieve those pressures—yoga, sports, and relaxation exercises—will pay off in a more fluid and powerful vocal instrument.

Getting to flow. Of course, in addition to being relaxed vocally, you must have something worthwhile to say. Neither beautiful words without meaning, nor the passionate delivery of a package empty of ideas will lead to success.

The power of your message, then, hinges on your ability to combine three things: message, vocal quality, and nonverbal communication. Like every good speaker, you must tie your material to your vocal delivery and body language, linking together three speech elements. Here's a sentence you can memorize that will help you remember this idea: *Fully commit to your message, express it passionately, and use supportive body language and gestures.* Who wouldn't be persuaded by such a speaker?

The voice is the perfect tool. Once you're aware of your personal potential for vocal power and expressiveness, you can learn how to more subtly influence your audience. For the *suppleness* of the vocal instrument is an important factor in persuading listeners that presenters too often ignore.

The voice, then, is the perfect tool for building trust; for instilling confidence in a product, service, or idea; for creating excitement among listeners; and for achieving other positive outcomes. But for these changes to occur, your audience must trust and respect you as a speaker. That means you need to have an honest conversation with your listeners, rather than "speechifying" or using your vocal powers to manipulate them.

The best way to sound natural and trustworthy to the people you want to influence is to start with a *vocal pitch* that's right for you.

EXERCISE 7-1

FINDING YOUR OPTIMAL PITCH

"Pitch" in terms of speech refers to the voice's highness or lowness on the musical scale. The size of one's vocal cords plays a role here, but so does the amount of tension present. The more tension in evidence, the higher the pitch will be because the vocal cords are tightened. Think of a guitar string: the more the string is "stopped" (shortened), the higher the musical note sounded will be.

Finding the pitch that's right for you is important, because the less tension you bring to your throat, the more relaxed your actual voice will be. For the sake of the exercise that follows, you also need one more piece of information: the terms habitual pitch and optimal pitch. We all speak at a certain pitch (highness or lowness) out of habit. However, sometimes that pitch puts a strain on our voice and prevents vocalization from being effortless (optimal) or from carrying far enough to reach our audience.

Males and females, for instance, sometimes use a habitual pitch that isn't optimal, for opposite reasons. Men can have a tendency to sit on their pitch, forcing it down into lower registers to sound more masculine; women can head in the opposite direction, using a light and girlish voice that may not match their maturity.

So, it's worth knowing whether the pitch you're in the habit of using is right for you in terms of vocal health and good sound production. Here are two quick-and-easy methods of FINDING YOUR OPTIMAL PITCH, regardless of the one you're using now out of habit:

METHOD #1

Without thinking about it beforehand, record yourself singing "Happy Birthday" (you can finish it with ". . . to Me" or anyone else's name!) Once you've sung "Happy Birthday," immediately record yourself talking about what your day has been like, using your normal voice. Now play back the two recordings. The song and the spoken passage should be at the same pitch, with neither one significantly higher or lower than the other. If they aren't, your rendition of "Happy Birthday" is closer to your optimal pitch, because singing it was spontaneous.

• •

METHOD #2

Sing a sustained note somewhere in the middle of your vocal range. Now "step down" one note on the musical scale at a time starting at the top, i.e., "Do," "Ti," "La," "So," and so on. Continue until you reach the lowest note you can sustain without your voice breaking up. Now come up two or three notes on the scale. That's your optimal pitch.

• •

If you just discovered that your habitual pitch (the one you're in the habit of using) doesn't match your optimal pitch (your healthiest and most effective pitch), make any necessary adjustments to get closer to your optimal pitch. Now remember to use your optimal pitch as often as possible. The idea is to eventually make speaking at that pitch your new habit!

THE 5 ESSENTIAL TOOLS OF VOCAL EXPRESSIVENESS

Now that you've found the pitch that's right for you, it's time to learn about the ingredients that will add variety and flavor to your voice. No one likes bland food, and the same principle applies to the vocal banquet you're serving up for your listeners.

There are many advantages to having a lively and expressive voice. They include audiences perceiving that you have more impact and power, as well as greater warmth, audibility, authority, trustworthiness, passion, intelligence, and assertiveness, among other attributes. Together these qualities will dramatically improve your ability to engage and influence listeners.

To achieve these qualities, you need to know about and use five essential vocal tools:

1. Emphasis and energy

2. Pitch inflection

3. Rhythm and pace

4. Pauses and silence

5. Vocal quality

Let's look at each of them in turn.

1. **Emphasis and energy** is concerned with the *force* or *stress* you place on important ideas, concepts, or feelings, as well as a generally energized vocal style. It is the simplest of the five essential vocal tools, and one that you probably already know how to use well.

2. **Pitch inflection** refers to the rising and falling of your pitch on the musical scale. Sometimes called *intonation*, lively pitch inflection helps you avoid monotony as well as convey meaning. It's not only a critically important vocal tool; it's the one you may have the most trouble using freely in formal speaking situations. If you haven't received performance training in the use of the voice, you may stay in a too-narrow pitch range, limiting your voice's natural ability to express emotion.

   If you find, for instance, that when you speak in public your voice has a 'flat' quality, it's possible that self-consciousness is inhibiting your ability to vary your pitch to convey emotional content. I'd be willing to bet that you don't use such an expressionless voice when you're telling a joke to friends or explaining to your spouse what's making you angry!

3. Your **rhythm and pace** also need to be varied when you speak publicly so your audience stays attentive and aware of the nuances of what you're saying. In normal conversation, i.e., when you're not self-conscious, your speaking rhythm changes frequently according to new ideas or emotions you bring up. Why should it be any different when you're giving a presentation? If you've ever suffered through a talk by a presenter who speaks in metronomic fashion, you know how an unvaried pace can lull an audience into inattention.

4. **Pauses and silence** is another vocal tool you may be neglecting due to speech anxiety. Pauses in a speech can add emphasis, build suspense, bridge ideas, make a comment on what you just said, and enrich your talk in other subtle ways. If you pause at appropriate times, you'll also show your audience that you're confident enough to set the pace for yourself rather than rushing through your talk because of nervousness. Unfortunately, adrenaline by its nature forces you to either fight the "threat" you're facing or run from it—in other words, taking any course of action rather than pausing!

    Pauses are also essential at two other times in your talk: when you've just said something important that needs time to sink in, and when you transition between main talking points. Ideas and information segments come together naturally when you speak, and by pausing before going on to something new, you allow your listeners to "take a mental breath" before your next critical piece of information.

5. **Vocal quality** is the most all-encompassing of the five vocal tools. It includes the tone, richness, and pleasantness of your voice, along with other factors such as breathiness, warmth or stridency, patience or impatience, empathy or anger, hesitancy or bewilderment, and other elements that affect people's emotional response when you speak. No wonder vocal quality is the most inclusive of the essential tools!

    Since it's the culminating effect that incorporates the other four tools, vocal quality is the most sophisticated vocal attribute in your toolbox. You might change your vocal quality, for instance, when you want to lead your audience to a certain emotional response—a whispered phrase to evoke mystery and suppressed emotion, or a doltish voice when you're characterizing a thick-headed person, etc.

The key to the five essential vocal tools is that they should be used *together* rather than in isolation, for that's when they work best. Now that you know what they are, use them all because they are fully and easily at your disposal at all times. Your audiences will stay tuned more easily, pay closer attention to what you're saying, and find themselves more easily moved and persuaded.

Now it's time for you to practice! The following exercises, of prose, poetry, and song include passages that are rich in opportunities for you to use all of the vocal tools. You'll probably also find that they're lots of fun to speak aloud.

EXERCISE 7-2

BOOSTING YOUR VOCAL IMPACT – USING THE 5 VOCAL TOOLS

The exercise that follows gives you a particularly rich opportunity to practice each of the tools of vocal expressiveness described above. In fact, you might say that you can really sink your teeth into this one, since it's from Bram Stoker's novel Dracula.

Novels and poetry are two of the best sources of material to help you improve your vocal dynamics. They combine compression of language with vivid imagery, giving you the chance to "paint word pictures" when you read them aloud. That of course is exactly what you need to do when speaking to an audience.

The following passage from Dracula has another advantage: the first-person narrator (you) experiences a dramatic emotional range in just three paragraphs. He travels all the way from calm contemplation of a moonlit night, to bewilderment and confusion, to awe, to sheer terror and fear for his life. It's a golden opportunity to make a character's inner life come to life through your spoken expression. Though you won't be acting out roles in your presentations, tapping into your emotional response—and eliciting such responses in your audience—is a key skill of effective public speaking.

First, some background: The narrator Jonathan Harker is a lawyer who has been sent to Transylvania to show a mysterious nobleman, Count Dracula, some London properties that the count is considering purchasing. Very shortly, however, Harker finds himself a prisoner in the count's ancient castle. In this diary entry,[14] he describes an unforgettable sight that freezes his soul.

You'll be reading that diary entry aloud. First, read the piece silently so you can understand what the passage is all about. It is evening, and Harker is standing at a window in his locked bedroom looking out at the landscape.

> I looked out over the beautiful expanse, bathed in soft yellow moonlight till it was almost as light as day. In the soft light the distant hills became melted, and the shadows in the val-

---

14 *Dracula* is an "epistolary" novel, a popular 18th and 19th-century literary form in which the entire story is told through diary entries, letters, or newspaper stories.

leys and gorges [were] of velvety blackness. The mere beauty seemed to cheer me; there was peace and comfort in every breath I drew. As I leaned from the window my eye was caught by something moving a story below me, and somewhat to my left, where I imagined, from the order of the rooms that the windows of the Count's own room would look out. The window at which I stood was tall and deep, stone-mullioned [pronounced "MULL-yunned"], and though weather worn, was still complete; but it was evidently many a day since the case had been there. I drew back behind the stonework, and looked carefully out.

What I saw was the Count's head coming out from the window. I did not see the face, but I knew the man by the neck and the movement of his back and arms. In any case I could not mistake the hands, which I had had so many opportunities of studying. I was at first interested and somewhat amused, for it is wonderful how small a matter will interest and amuse a man when he is a prisoner. But my very feelings changed to repulsion and terror when I saw the whole man slowly emerge from the window and begin to crawl down the castle wall over that dreadful abyss, *face down*, with his cloak spreading out around him like great wings. At first I could not believe my eyes. I thought it was some trick of the moonlight, some weird effect of shadow; but I kept looking, and it could be no delusion. I saw the fingers and toes grasp the corners of the stones, worn clear of the mortar by the stress of years, and by thus using every projection and inequality move downwards with considerable speed, just as a lizard moves along a wall.

What manner of man is this, or what manner of creature is it in the semblance of man? I feel the dread of this horrible place overpowering me; I am in fear—in awful fear—and there is no escape for me.

From *Dracula*, by Bram Stoker

Did you notice the transitions in this passage—the places where the mood, idea, or images change? Transitions point to places where your vocal "flavor" needs to be different. The need for your voice to reflect the changing ideas or emotions of your content is as basic to business and professional communication as it is to novels and dramatic literature. Let's look at the same excerpt from Dracula, this time focusing on the transitions. There are four major transitions resulting in five distinct sections of content. I've indicated those separations below:

> I looked out over the beautiful expanse, bathed in soft yellow moonlight till it was almost as light as day. In the soft light the distant hills became melted, and the shadows in the valleys and gorges [were] of velvety blackness. The mere beauty seemed to cheer me; there was peace and comfort in every breath I drew.
>
> •
>
> As I leaned from the window my eye was caught by something moving a story below me, and somewhat to my left, where I imagined, from the order of the rooms that the windows of the Count's own room would look out. The window at which I stood was tall and deep, stone-mullioned, and though weather worn, was still complete; but it was evidently many a day since the case had been there. I drew back behind the stonework, and looked carefully out.
>
> •
>
> What I saw was the Count's head coming out from the window. I did not see the face, but I knew the man by the neck and the movement of his back and arms. In any case I could not mistake the hands which I had had so many opportunities of studying. I was at first interested and somewhat amused, for it is wonderful how small a matter will interest and amuse a man when he is a prisoner.
>
> •
>
> But my very feelings changed to repulsion and terror when I saw the whole man slowly emerge from the window and begin to

crawl down the castle wall over that dreadful abyss, *face down*, with his cloak spreading out around him like great wings. At first I could not believe my eyes. I thought it was some trick of the moonlight, some weird effect of shadow; but I kept looking, and it could be no delusion. I saw the fingers and toes grasp the corners of the stones, worn clear of the mortar by the stress of years, and by thus using every projection and inequality move downwards with considerable speed, just as a lizard moves along a wall.

. . . .

What manner of man is this, or what manner of creature is it in the semblance of man? I feel the dread of this horrible place overpowering me; I am in fear—in awful fear—and there is no escape for me.

Speak the passage aloud, using one of the vocal tools. *Now that you've made sense of this selection from Dracula and you're aware of the transitions, go ahead and speak the piece out loud. As you do so, consciously use one of the 5 essential tools of vocal expressiveness: emphasis and energy, pitch inflection, rhythm and pace, pauses and silence, or vocal quality. Read the passage aloud giving particular focus to one of those tools.*[15]

Now use all of the vocal tools. *Speak the selection again, this time allowing your voice to fully reflect what you are thinking and feeling at each stage as you describe these incredible events. This is not acting since you're not being asked to become Harker in a stage performance, but it is employing the actor's toolbox of a fully expressive and active voice.*

Passages like this one that are written well enough to portray strong human thoughts and emotions can help you bring more liveliness and energy to your speech. The freedom of expression you gain will give you confidence that you are, indeed, an interesting speaker.

---

15 Please understand that proceeding this way is only for the purpose of this exercise. When you're speaking in front of an audience, you should use *all* the tools of vocal dynamics. Only in that way will your voice reflect the richness of the thoughts, emotions, and intentions embodied in your content

EXERCISE 7-3

BRINGING IDEAS AND EMOTIONS TO LIFE

Now let's add another key element to your effectiveness as a speaker. This technique is an outgrowth of your work in Chapter Three on controlled breathing.

As you know from that chapter, controlling your breath is critical to countering the effects of speech fright. Pronounced nervousness almost always disrupts the breathing rhythm as it introduces psychological distress. And if your breathing is disrupted, the flow of ideas and emotions in what you're saying will be broken. To prevent this from happening, you need to learn how to support the sound you're producing so the ENDS OF PHRASES come through clearly to your listeners.

Here's why this is important: In speech (rather than written communication), you don't speak sentences; you speak ideas and emotions. So you have to sustain the produced sound until you reach the end of the idea you're trying to express. In fact, you can get into trouble if you think in terms of sentences (as they're written in your notes) rather than the idea you're trying to convey. For example, an idea may take three sentences to be expressed, while another sentence may contain three different ideas, and so on.

Now for the other part of the equation.

In English, the most important word usually comes at the END of the phrase.

That's the payoff for listeners, and that's why you need to speak the end of that phrase emphatically, with full breath support. For example, let's look at the most famous line of Shakespeare's—"To be, or not to be: that is the QUESTION." That "question" is the whole point of Hamlet delivering this soliloquy, and it comes at the end of the phrase he speaks.

Imagine an actor who loses his breath in the middle of this all-important pronouncement! What the audience member hears, and his or her response would be something like this:

> *Hamlet:* To be or not to be, that is the question . . . .
>
> *Audience Member:* Huh? What was that? George [Debbie], did you hear what he said?

Something would be rotten in Denmark indeed in such a performance!

What does all of this have to do with the presentation or speech you'll be giving? Well, let's look at some current-day examples from the worlds of business, politics, and sports to see why supporting an idea vocally is a good idea. The italics are mine, added to point out how the important ideas in these quotes occur at the ends of phrases:

- *"Tonight, all of our men and women in uniform—in Iraq, Afghanistan and around the world—must know that they have our respect, our gratitude, and our full support."*[16]

- *"Now, in many respects, information has never been so free. There are more ways to spread more ideas to more people than at any moment in history."*[17]

- *"Are we ready for tomorrow, today? For the next day and a half, you're going to see, first-hand, how we are shaping the future—today."*[18]

- *"One of my goals has always been never to work a day in my life. I don't consider what I do as work, because every day that I train and compete, I find even greater joy in the process."*[19]

---

16 Barack Obama, President of the United States of America, State of the Union Speech (January 27, 2010).

17 Hillary Clinton, Secretary of State, United States of America, "Remarks on Internet Freedom," Newseum, Washington, D.C. (January 21, 2010).

18 Muhtar Kent, President and CEO, The Coca-Cola Co., "Are We Ready for Tomorrow, Today?" Investor and Analyst Event, The World of Coca-Cola, Atlanta, GA (November 16, 2009).

19 Yael Averbuch, Midfielder, Sky Blue FC women's professional soccer team, "Love the Process," National Soccer Coaches Association of America Women's Soccer Breakfast, Philadelphia, PA (January 21, 2010). This excerpt and the previous excerpts are taken from *Vital Speeches of the Day* LXXVI No. 3 (March 2010): 98-127.

You can see how the force of an idea is amplified when it occurs at the end of a phrase. It resonates in listeners' minds, therefore, in the second or two before the next phrase is spoken. Obviously, if an audience is to receive the full force and impact of what you're saying, your words must be supported with breathing that can "punch" up that word or phrase.

To make sure you're supporting your own sound in this way, practice your diaphragmatic breathing again. If you need to, go back to Exercise 3-3, "Diaphragmatic Breathing," to regain your ability to get a full reservoir of nourishing oxygen to support vocal production.

Absolutely the best examples of this effect in action are the speeches delivered by Shakespeare's characters. Let's look at why this is the case.

Shakespeare and his contemporaries wrote their verse (as they described their dramatic writing) in iambic pentameter. That term simply means a poetic line consisting of five "feet" or measures, each of which incorporates a short-long accent, like this: "To be or not to be, that is the question." (The non-italicized words contain the accent.[20])

The Elizabethan dramatists chose iambic pentameter for their characters' speech because it mimics real speech. It's the form of poetic diction that sounds most like the way we really talk.

Try speaking aloud the following passages from Shakespeare and you'll hear it right away. Don't be intimidated by the fact that these lines were written in the late 16th century: the ideas and emotions expressed are as current as the thought you had a moment ago. Make sure you take a deep enough breath so you have the vocal energy necessary to punch up the italicized words (you needn't punch up the titles of the plays, which also happen to be italicized). Again, except for the titles the italics are my own:

20 The extra syllable on the word "question" is of little importance here.

- In King Henry IV, Part One, the Earl of Douglas, fighting with the rebels, encounters Sir Walter Blunt,[21] who to confuse the enemy is disguised in the armor of King Henry IV. Douglas naturally believes he has found the king, whom he intends to slay on the battlefield: (One breath only now:)

Know then, my name is Douglas;
And I do haunt thee in the battle thus
Because some tell me that *thou art a king*.

- In a famous scene from The Taming of the Shrew, Petruchio, a gentleman of Verona visiting Padua, decides to woo Katharine, the "shrew" or unpleasant female of the title. Though famous for her temper, Katharine or "Kate" possesses a large dowry. Petruchio is delighted by both the challenge and the lady's riches, and vows that he will win Kate for his wife. What follows is their first encounter (you can speak both parts). Even at their first meeting, the air is electric with sexual tension. Their repartee is therefore filled with double entendres and racy references. This time I haven't italicized the operative words at the ends of phrases—go ahead and find them yourself:

Petruchio: Come, come, you wasp; i' faith, you are too angry.

Katharine: If I be waspish, best beware my sting.

Petruchio: My remedy is then, to pluck it out.

Katharine: Ay, if the fool could find it where it lies.

Petruchio: Who knows not where a wasp does wear his sting?
            In his tail.

Katharine: In his tongue.

Petruchio: Whose tongue?

Katharine: Yours, if you talk of tails; and so farewell.

Petruchio: What, with my tongue in your tail? nay, come again,
            Good Kate; I am a gentleman.

Katharine: That I'll try [i.e., test].

She strikes him.

21 I once portrayed Sir Walter in an Off-Broadway production of this play and, yes, was fated to die with little fanfare. Immediately after I came on stage, I might add.

You don't have to actually hit yourself in this exercise!

Notice the words at the ends of the lines in this scene: ANGRY, STING, PLUCK IT OUT, LIES, TAIL, TONGUE, TONGUE, FAREWELL, COME AGAIN, GENTLEMAN, TRY (followed by the slap). Believe me, audiences have no difficulty, 400-year-old dialogue or not, understanding the flirting and sexual challenges flying back and forth in this scene.

- *Our final selection is from Romeo and Juliet. Romeo, having overcome his schoolboy crush on another girl, realizes that Juliet, the daughter of his family's sworn enemies, is the young lady he is destined to love. Hiding in the Capulets' orchard at night, he sees Juliet appear at a window. His soliloquy, incidentally, is an ideal piece to use for "supporting your words." It is simple and straightforward, yet suffused with young passion; and the important phrases are clearly delineated at the end of each line. Give these words the clarity and emphasis they demand through your voice. This speech will then not only live, but it will be Romeo Montague who speaks through the rhythms and emphases Shakespeare has fashioned.[22]*

But, soft! what light through yonder window breaks?
It is the east, and Juliet is the sun.
Arise, fair sun, and kill the envious moon,
Who is already sick and pale with grief,
That thou her maid art far more fair than she:
Be not her maid, since she is envious;
Her vestal livery is but sick and green
And none but fools do wear it; cast it off.
It is my lady, O, it is my love!
O, that she knew she were!
She speaks yet she says nothing: what of that?
Her eye discourses; I will answer it.
I am too bold, 'tis not to me she speaks:
Two of the fairest stars in all the heaven,
Having some business, do entreat her eyes

---

22 Shakespeare's plays are always a delight to act in, because he's a genius at constructing dialogue in a way that captures and portrays the personality of each individual character. In a way, one doesn't have to do much when acting Shakespeare except speak the lines he's given you as an actor.

To twinkle in their spheres till they return.
What if her eyes were there, they in her head?
The brightness of her cheek would shame those stars,
As daylight doth a lamp; her eyes in heaven
Would through the airy region stream so bright
That birds would sing and think it were not night.
See, how she leans her cheek upon her hand!
O, that I were a glove upon that hand,
That I might touch that cheek!

This exercise should make you aware of how emotions and ideas have prominence because of their position in your phrases and remarks. It isn't necessary for you to intentionally place important words at the ends of utterances—the language you speak, English, has already placed them there for you.

Apply what you've just practiced to your speeches and presentations. Notice that, more often than not, the thing you say as you conclude a phrase or idea has importance, and you should make sure your listeners hear it clearly. Don't let your voice sink as you complete a phrase and get ready for the next idea (a common mistake of speakers). The idea you're still expressing needs to come across with clarity and power to your audience.

EXERCISE 7-4

THE 3-MINUTE SPEECH WARM-UP

Have you noticed improvement in your vocal skills through the tools and techniques described above? If you've practiced the exercises, you're already developing a more flexible and dynamic speaking voice. That's an absolutely key skill for any presenter. Far more than any other asset you own, your voice is a responsive tool, only awaiting your skill in using it.

Now that you understand how your voice can affect listeners, you can use your instrument to achieve a wide range of colorations and effects. You can sound somber or light-hearted, for instance; cajoling or compelling; skeptical or inspirational; solicitous or powerful. By linking your intentions with your delivery skills, you can employ your full vocal range and virtuosity to drive home your critical messages.

One more point you should consider: vocal production is a physical process. Just as with any other muscle group, the vocal cords need to be warmed up to perform at their best. But with today's hectic professional schedules, getting in an adequate workout can be a challenge.

The solution is a vocal warm-up that takes just three minutes. Here is one I've put together. It covers the following trio of essential skills (and it should be done in this order):

(1) Breathing and resonance;

(2) Supporting the sound; and

(3) Warming up the articulators.

The three-minute warm-up is given on the following page.

. . . .

STEP ONE: BREATHING & RESONANCE

- Stand comfortably with your feet at armpit width apart. Close your eyes. Take three slow, deep breaths. Imagine your breath as both nourishment and relaxing energy.

- Focus on your abdominal area. Feel your belly come out at inhalation, and go back in when you exhale. As you now know, this is healthy controlled breathing: diaphragmatic or natural breathing.

STEP TWO: SUPPORTING AND SUSTAINING THE SOUND

- Breathe in slowly through your mouth to a silent count of five. Retain the breath for a silent count of five; then exhale gently to a silent count of five. Do this five times.

- Choosing a comfortable pitch, produce the sustained sound "ahh." You should produce this sound quietly and gently, without attacking the vowel. At the same time, think of "placing" the sound at a spot five to ten feet away from you—as though you were painting a dab of sound with a paintbrush. Don't "slide" up to the note. You're striking a balance: not getting up to the note sloppily, but not attacking it by making the sound harsh.

STEP THREE: WARMING UP THE ARTICULATORS

- Using your fingers, manipulate your facial muscles as if they were made of rubber. Practice chewing a huge imaginary wad of bubble gum with your lips closed but your teeth apart.

- Stick your tongue out and rotate it in wide circles. Blow your lips outward in a floppy "horsey" sound.

- Practice an articulation exercise, as in the samples below.

. . . .

ARTICULATION EXERCISES

Here is some fun material to further warm up those articulators: your lips, tongue, and facial muscles. The pieces below are "patter songs" from Gilbert and Sullivan operettas. Use these selections, tongue twisters, or anything similarly challenging as the last step before you speak so your diction is sharp, clear, and crisp.

From Trial by Jury:

> When I, good friends, was called to the bar
> I'd an appetite fresh and hearty.
> But I was, as many young barristers are
> An impecunious party.
> I'd a swallow-tail coat of a beautiful blue
> And a brief which I bought of a booby;
> A couple of shirts, and a collar or two
> And a ring that looked like a ruby.

> At Westminster Hall I danced a dance
> Like a semi-despondent fury;
> For I thought I never should hit on a chance
> Of addressing a British jury.
> But I soon got tired of third-class journeys
> And dinners of bread and water;
> So I fell in love with a rich attorney's
> Elderly, ugly daughter.

> The rich attorney, he jump'd with joy
> And replied to my fond professions:
> "You shall reap the reward of your pluck, my boy
> At the Bailey and Middlesex Sessions.
> You'll soon get used to her looks," said he
> "And a very nice girl you will find her;
> She may very well pass for forty-three
> In the dusk, with a light behind her!"

From Iolanthe:

When you're lying awake
With a dismal headache,
And repose is tabooed by anxiety,
I conceive you may use
Any language you choose
To indulge in, without impropriety;
For your brain is on fire,
And the bedclothes conspire
Of your usual slumber to plunder you:
First your counterpane goes,
And uncovers your toes,
And your sheet slips demurely from under you;
Then the blanketing tickles,
You feel like mixed pickles,
So terribly sharp is the pricking,
And you're hot, and you're cross,
And you tumble and toss
Till there's nothing 'twixt you and the ticking.
Then the bedclothes all creep
To the ground in a heap,
And you pick 'em all up in a tangle;
Next your pillow resigns
And politely declines
To remain at its usual angle!
Well, you get some repose
In the form of a doze,
With hot eye-balls and head ever aching.
But your slumbering teems
With such horrible dreams
That you'd very much better be waking.

And *this famous selection from* The Pirates of Penzance:

I am the very model of a modern Major-General,
I've information vegetable[23], animal, and mineral,
I know the kings of England, and I quote the fights historical
From Marathon to Waterloo, in order categorical;
I'm very well acquainted, too, with matters mathematical,
I understand equations, both the simple and quadratical,
About binomial theorem I'm teeming with a lot o' news,
With many cheerful facts about the square of the hypotenuse.
I'm very good at integral and differential calculus;
I know the scientific names of beings animalculous:
In short, in matters vegetable, animal, and mineral,
I am the very model of a modern Major-General.

---

23 That's pronounced with four syllables, "VEG-E-TA-BLE," to keep the scansion or meter of the verse.

RACHEL

Rachel is the Director of Field Resources for a healthcare provider. The organization has offices around the globe, and Rachel travels frequently to speak to her "country teams." When she first came to me she was only four months into her job, a position she had worked extremely hard to be promoted to from within the organization.

Rachel is the type of person who, despite a demanding schedule, prepares her presentations meticulously, but she wasn't feeling like herself when she spoke. She realized she was just trying to *get through* her presentations rather than making the impact she desired. She believed she was at a disadvantage because she was young and female—the first woman, in fact, to be appointed to the position.

She was compensating for the situation, as she perceived it by trying to sound stronger, i.e., by pushing down on her voice to make it deeper and more masculine. Of course, she had no limitations in terms of talent or ability that would make any of this necessary, but she appeared to believe subconsciously that she would be taken more seriously if she had a deeper and more resonant voice.

I worked with her specifically to "lighten" her tone: to stop tightening her vocal cords to produce a deeper sound. That wasn't her real voice. In fact, her staff was being short-changed by not hearing the person who actually had been hired for the job! Through audio- and video-taping, Rachel eventually realized that her lighter and more feminine voice wasn't a hindrance at all—it was one of her strengths. Her humor and sheer humanity came through much more clearly when she spoke in her actual voice, rather than trying to sound like someone whom she wasn't in real life.

8

USING POSITIVE VISUALIZATION

Do you golf? Ski? Enjoy chess? When you're about to have a serious discussion with your spouse or your boss, do you imagine how the conversation will go? Or when you're driving home at night, do you anticipate in your mind's eye that curve in the road you know is ahead so you can slow down in time?

In these situations and others, chances are you *visualize* the best way to proceed to give yourself an edge.

To speak successfully, you need to use the exact same technique. Visualizing giving an effective presentation makes it easier to achieve that result. As I often say to clients: If you're going to spend the time and energy to think ahead about an upcoming speech, why not make your effort productive instead of destructive?

One of the best ways to do this is through a technique called *positive visualization*. This chapter of *Fearless Speaking* explains the technique and gives you some opportunities to practice.

Up until now in this book, you've learned some key techniques for confident public speaking: cognitive restructuring, diaphragmatic breathing, body language, achieving stage presence, and using vocal dynamics. Now you're ready to "assemble" these elements by visualizing how you'll use all of these tools successfully. It's a logical step and a hugely important one.

First, let's look at how positive visualization works.

THE POWER OF A SELF-FULFILLING PROPHECY

Do you know about the white lines on the highway? When you're driving, one of the worst things you can do is to focus on the painted lines in the center of the road. If you stare at those lines long enough, you'll begin drifting *toward* them, i.e., close to or into the path of oncoming traffic. By directing your energy and attention toward the lines, you'll have created an attraction between you and them. After that, it's just a case of you following your attraction.

Another way to say this is: *When you create the right conditions for something to happen it's much more likely for that outcome to take place.* In effect, you're preparing for the event subconsciously and getting yourself ready to respond to it.

Now consider all of this in terms of public speaking. When you have an important presentation coming up, naturally you think about it a lot. Even if you're not particularly anxious concerning the outcome, you'll still give it plenty of "mind time." And if you're prone to speaking anxiety, the chances are excellent that you'll create negative scenarios about what's going to take place.

At that point, you're in danger of creating a self-fulfilling prophecy. By establishing the right conditions, you're heading toward—and in a sense inviting—the very outcome you don't want to occur.

You should also know that this is not a passive process. It takes a lot of work to undermine yourself as a speaker! But if you recognize the nature of self-fulfilling prophecies and accept your own power to head them off, you can put yourself back on the path to speaking success.

The following pages offer six exercises to help you do so. These scenarios are specifically designed to "lighten your load" in terms of public speaking anxiety while placing you in a more positive frame of mind.

From there, it's just a case of allowing the beneficial outcomes to take place!

EXERCISE 8-1

THE BALLOON MAN/LADY

In this first exercise, you'll start by filling yourself up with . . .

Nothing.

That's right: Imagine a feeling of complete and total emptiness. Notice how utterly light this makes you. Weighty matters no longer burden you. You're now light enough, in fact, to float away.

What you're experiencing by imagining the above is not just playfulness but a serious concept from Zen Buddhism—a philosophy which aims to "liberate us from all the yokes under which we finite beings are usually suffering in this world."[24]

The particular burden you're attempting to get out from under, of course, is your public speaking anxiety. Weighty thoughts, heavy breathing, and the pressure you place on your own shoulders— these are the encumbrances that may accompany your important speeches and presentations.

But right now, you're letting all of that go as you reach a state of emptiness.

You're free. And so . . . UP you float.

You're completely empty; remember? You're the Balloon Man or Balloon Lady, floating above the heads of everyone. Breathe in and you go higher. Exhale and you float a little lower.

Imagine: you can be as light as you want just by breathing! You're released.

Float over to your office now or the place where you'll be giving your next speech. Everything certainly looks different from up here doesn't it?

Nothing at all, even high-stakes presentations, has any weight for the Balloon Man or Balloon Lady.

Can you use this exercise to lighten your frame of mind just before a speech or presentation?

Why n t?

24   D.T. Suzuki, *Zen Buddhism*, William Barrett, ed. (New York: Three Leaves Press, 2006), 3.

EXERCISES 8-2 AND 8-3

THE NEUTRAL MASK AND THE ACTOR'S BOX

Here are two visualization techniques from the theater that can help reduce your speaking anxiety: the Neutral Mask and the Actor's Box. Though very different in approach, both techniques harness the power of performance to help make you a more confident and focused speaker.

The Neutral Mask. This device is exactly what it sounds like: a human mask that displays no expression whatever. It's typically a light mask made out of leather or neoprene, secured with an elastic band that fits over the back of the wearer's head. The following is a description of the neutral mask's purpose:

> The Neutral Mask doesn't have any dramatic expression, and allows the actor to explore a state of *pure presence*, in the here and now of space. With this mask the actor explores the state of neutrality that exists *before the action*. . . . It lives in the present, and allows the actor to explore economy of movement (italics added).[25]

The neutral mask is a mask of calmness that exists only in the present.[26] This means that the performer wearing the mask embodies tremendous potential: nothing is happening yet or is preordained; everything is possible from this point on.

Consider: by entering such a state if you have speaking anxiety, your performance can be fresh and without strain. There is no self-fulfilling prophecy of failure waiting in the wings! The world of the presentation you're about to give is yours to populate with new hope and promise. Wearing the neutral mask, you can truly start out in a neutral state, unburdened by any presentations (yours or those of others) that have gone before.

For the purpose of this exercise, you needn't buy a neutral mask from a theatrical supplier. Just assume as neutral an expression as you can manage. For just as emotions elicit physical responses (when you're confused you frown, when you're surprised your

---

25 Giovanni Fusetti, "The Neutral Mask – The Silence Before the Drama," on http://www.giovannifusetti.com/public/file/lecture_neutral.pdf, accessed January 31, 2011.

26 "Neutral Mask," on http://www.theater-masks.com/neutral-masks, accessed January 31, 2011.

eyes open wide, etc.), the opposite works as well—by taking on a sad expression, you'll actually feel sadder, and so on.

Now imagine you're about to deliver a speech. Just before you begin, slip on your "neutral mask." Your features now demonstrate no emotion (and vice versa). Because your face is set in a neutral mode, you're neither thinking about the past nor anticipating anything that's about to happen: you're completely in the present. You occupy an instant of limitless potential.

What a marvelous place to be in just before you speak! From your neutral starting place, power, control, and dynamism can only grow.

The Actor's Box. This exercise calls for a completely different approach. Instead of inhabiting a neutral place without thought or intention, you'll be consciously thinking about matters that are likely to intrude upon your focus and awareness.

The Actor's Box is an imaginary item: a small cabinet that you lock with a tiny key. Make the cabinet small enough in your imagination that you could carry it with you if it actually existed as a solid object. Actors use this box as a temporary home for all the little demon-thoughts from their personal lives that are apt to nip at them and spoil their performance.

You'll be using the box in the same way to keep your speech or presentation focused. The idea is for you to practice this technique now, then bring along your "box" and use it just before your next public speaking appearance. Here's what to do:

- Five or ten minutes before you're about to speak, find a private quiet place. Set the imaginary box down next to you.

- Turn the invisible key and open the door.

- Now spend a few moments with the things that are on your mind or bothering you today. The nature of the thought or worry doesn't matter. It simply needs to be something that you don't want to bring on stage with you when you're presenting.

- Validate that worry or concern by thinking about it for 15 seconds or so. In other words, give it a little attention. If you need to make a decision on this matter, tell yourself that you will make a decision . . . later. Once you've spent some time with each individual concern or worry, place it in the box.

- Repeat the procedure for up to six things that you'd rather not have on your mind, as you're about to speak.

- Close the door to your imaginary box, and lock it. Put the "key" in a safe place.

- Your worries are now safely inside your Actor's Box. Since you've given each of them a little time and attention (which they were clamoring for), they'll stay quiet for the hour or so that you'll be speaking. They'll behave themselves for a while. If on the other hand you had ignored or repressed them, they may have intruded on your thoughts when you could least afford to have them do so. Instead, they're taking a nice nap and won't bother you.

- If you forget to go back to the box and let them out after your presentation, don't worry. They're determined little critters and they'll find their way back to you with no trouble whatsoever.

EXERCISE 8-4

THE SPOTLIGHT TECHNIQUES

The visualizations already discussed are designed to get you into a positive state of mind prior to speaking. The next two exercises, by contrast, are for calming and centering you during your speeches and presentations.

They're called the "Spotlight Techniques," and you have a choice as to which of them to practice. Of course, you can try them both. Some of my clients say that the Spotlight Techniques are the most helpful visualizations they learn to help overcome in-the-moment public speaking fear. But you can judge for yourself. Whichever approaches among those introduced in this chapter work for you are the visualizations you should use.

The first Spotlight Technique is meant to be a completely practical and hands-on technique, and it also comes from the world of the theater. I find the second Spotlight Technique to be more spiritual in nature, and you may too.

SPOTLIGHT TECHNIQUE #1

When you're overly nervous and anxious as a public speaker, you place yourself in a "third degree" spotlight. That's the name for the harsh bright light police detectives used in days gone by to "sweat" a suspect and elicit a confession. An interrogation room was always otherwise dimly lit, so the source of light trained on the person (who was usually forced to sit in a hard straight-backed chair) was unrelenting.

This spotlight is always harsh, hot, and uncomfortable—and the truth is, you voluntarily train it on yourself by believing your audience is unforgiving. The larger the audience, the more likely you believe that to be true.

So here's a technique to get out from under this hot spotlight that you're imagining so vividly: turn it around! Visualize swiveling the spotlight so it's aimed at your audience instead of at you. After all, aren't you supposed to illuminate your listeners? You don't want to leave them in the dark, do you?

There's no doubt that it's cooler and much more comfortable when you're out from under that harsh light. The added benefit is that now the light is shining on your listeners—without question the most important people in the room or auditorium!

SPOTLIGHT TECHNIQUE #2

This technique is a variation of the one above. Rather than visualizing a bright spotlight beaming down on you, imagine that a gentle light is shining from WITHIN you. You're no longer being subjected to the third degree. Instead—and much more importantly—YOU are the source of the light.

Your knowledge, expertise, sympathy, and goodwill glow from within you, bathing and embracing your listeners. Far from producing anxiety, this visualization should leave you feeling warm and generous to both yourself and your audience.

EXERCISE 8-5

WRITING YOUR FEARS AWAY

Ready for an entirely different type of visualization?

So far in this chapter, you've been sampling ways to reduce your level of anxiety by focusing away your fears. Now you're going to embrace those fears—to face them honestly and benefit from doing so.

There's a scientific basis for such a counter-intuitive approach. It's from a recent study. Students, who were allowed to write about their anxiety before a test, actually reduced the loss of performance caused by nerves.

Subjects in this experiment, along with real high-school biology test-takers, were asked either to sit quietly for ten minutes before a test, or write about their anxiety. The result? The non-writers' test scores dropped by an average of 12 percentage points, while the "anxiety writers" raised their scores by four percentage points.[27]

So that's your assignment right now: For the next fifteen minutes, write about your public speaking fears. Try not to conceptualize. Instead, write down your actual emotional responses. Also avoid rationalizing or trying to make sense of your description, for fear often has no rational component.

It's possible that you might actually enjoy not trying to fight your public speaking anxiety for once. You'll be welcoming it instead, sitting down with it and having a chat!

Why would such an approach work? I believe it's because the activity is akin to the Actor's Box exercise above. In both cases, you're giving your fears and worries some attention—some face time, if you will. After their experience being hidden away in dark recesses of your mind, it must be refreshing for them to see the light of day.

Also of course, in the daylight they don't look so scary. They're your fears, after all—in existence only because you've given them life. Acknowledging them and coming to terms with them may

---

27   "Writing Your Fears Away," *Wall Street Journal*, January 22-23, 2011. I have adopted the title of the article for this visualization exercise.

help you manage their disruptive behavior. Maybe now they'll be better behaved.

So try "Writing Your Fears Away" before you deliver a presentation that's causing you anxiety. If it helps, add the exercise to your public speaking toolbox.

EXERCISE 8-6

YOUR COMMAND PERFORMANCE MOVIE

Do you remember the concepts of "Worst-Case Thinking" and "awfulizing" from Chapter Two?

Here are those descriptions again:

"Worst-Case Thinking" means imagining that a truly bad outcome is going to take place despite a lack of any evidence. And "awfulizing" is making such an adverse event the scenario you visualize (and subconsciously prepare for) in advance of your speech.

Doesn't it make more sense to visualize a positive outcome to your presentation?

If you have public speaking anxiety, you probably don't need to be told that you can be your own worst enemy concerning what might happen in a stressful situation. It's time to leave such unproductive behavior behind and give yourself a head start toward success.

One way to do so is by preparing what I call a **Command Performance Movie.**

A Command Performance Movie isn't a real movie shot with a camcorder. It's a scenario that you write out to help you visualize a beneficial outcome to your speech or presentation. As you now know, doing so should actually help predispose you toward the result you're looking for.

You'll be writing a page or two that describes your upcoming speaking situation. Some of the details you should mention include the following:

- Your pleasure about speaking on this occasion.

- Your accomplishment of all of your objectives in this speech.

- Your audience's pleasure and attentiveness (including the nods and smiles you notice).

- Your success in getting the audience to perceive you the way you want them to.

- Your own positive impressions and feelings about the experience.

Will all of this come to pass exactly as you're writing it now? Of course not. You're not a fortune-teller, after all. The point is to give yourself a positive and upbeat scenario that's more likely to occur if you're actively preparing for such a result.

Here's a further hint on how to make your Command Performance Movie productive: avoid dry descriptions such as, "I deliver the presentation with last month's sales figures." Well, yes, you do, but will writing that down really help you? Instead, include your emotional experiences and that of others: "I hear the boss say 'Wow!' as I show the animated slide comparing last year's sales figures with this year's." That's a detail that will help put you in a positive frame of mind!

Remember, your public speaking anxiety is emotionally based. Your visualization, therefore, should focus on some emotional reward from your performance.

A sample Command Performance Movie that I created is given below as an example. Yours will be different, since it will be unique to your situation and goals. Also, the example below is somewhat brief since it's only meant to give you the flavor of the exercise. Your movie should go into more specifics.

Make your imagined scenario as close to the actual situation as you believe it will unfold. The purpose of the exercise isn't predictive—it's to "remind" yourself of what an enjoyable emotional experience your presentation is going to be for you.

MY COMMAND PERFORMANCE MOVIE

Today, I'm giving the keynote address at the Mega-Movers of the Universe Convention. I'm really looking forward to this occasion. This is an important group, and I've prepared extensively to give them something dynamic and interesting.

Earlier this week, I put the finishing touches on my talk. Last night I got a good night's sleep, and I had a healthy breakfast this morning. I'm feeling good! I've also allowed myself plenty of time to get to the venue, so I'm not rushed. And it's been nice to have a few minutes to meet the people coming into the hotel ballroom and to introduce myself. Now I'll no longer be talking to strangers!

I'm dressed professionally, in style with good quality clothes that aren't overly flashy. The audience senses that I'm relaxed, confident, and clearly looking forward to giving my talk and sharing ideas with them.

In fact, they can see I'm really enjoying the opportunity to speak to this group. After I'm introduced, I step to the lectern, smile, and nod to the audience. I take a slow relaxed breath, and begin my conversation with my listeners.

I speak clearly and knowledgeably in an easy, confident tone. My voice is lively and engaging. As I make eye contact with audience members, I see that they're paying attention and looking interested. I stay focused on my message, which I know is coming through loud and clear. I know this material and I'm enjoying getting it across.

When I finish, everyone smiles and applauds warmly. They've clearly enjoyed my speech. As I return to my seat I overhear someone say, "Now THAT was an interesting presentation!" I know this has been a rewarding experience for them *and* me.

CHO

Cho was convinced that she turned people off when she spoke. She was born in Japan but moved to the U.S. at age ten. Because she was a native speaker of Japanese, she was certain that people found her English difficult to understand. She was like other educated non-native speakers whose English is flawless, but who still think audiences focus on their *inability* to pronounce words correctly. Cho was convinced that when she presented or participated in phone conferences, people "only hear my accent."

Because of this belief, she didn't enjoy her presentations and conference calls on behalf of her Internet security company. Instead, she was preparing for failure. She would imagine scenarios in which numerous objections and resistance would arise—all due to her perceived inability to communicate well. She also believed that people would make the leap from her poor communication skills into thinking that she wasn't a good project manager.

The Actor's Box (Exercise 8-3 in this chapter) was the first visualization technique I used with Cho. This was because apart from her lack of confidence, she faced constant "small fires" at work that intruded on her ability to stay focused. The Actor's Box allowed her to set aside the items that were important but not really related to the topic she was speaking on.

From there, it was a small step to getting Cho to use other techniques of positive visualization. "Seeing" a positive outcome in her mind meant that her actual presentations had a much greater chance of succeeding the way she wanted them to.

9

REDUCING NERVOUSNESS WHILE YOU'RE SPEAKING

In the last chapter of *Fearless Speaking*, you learned about using a self-fulfilling prophecy to "create your own success" as a speaker. The visualizations you practiced were designed to put you in the right frame of mind prior to speaking rather than focusing on your anxiety.

Now you'll go one important step further—to reduce your nervousness *while you're speaking*. The exercises in this chapter are specifically designed to address the self-consciousness that leads to feelings of exposure and to "speaking nerves." Their goal is to bring you out of yourself so you're more comfortable in front of others. They will help you to become more audience-centered: the mark of a confident and influential speaker.

THE SELF-CONSCIOUS PRESENTER

If you suffer from stage fright, it's most likely true that you deal with powerful feelings of self-consciousness while presenting. And no wonder! Facing audiences small or large armed only with one's personality and message is a level of exposure that would make nearly anyone uncomfortable.

And even though deep down you realize that public speaking isn't dangerous, it still *feels* that way. Once you're in the grip of performance anxiety, the realization of your own vulnerability can crowd out every other consideration—including what you're trying to achieve with listeners.

Then there's the sheer size of your audience. Like most people, you're probably at ease in fairly intimate settings, talking to individuals or small groups. Think of speaking with family members or your team at the office, for instance. In these situations, it's as though you were sitting around a campfire telling stories (which, in evolutionary terms, I believe we're all still programmed to do).

A large audience in a formal speech or presentation, on the other hand, is another matter. Even though such groups are often made up of the same people you talk to in smaller gatherings without any self-consciousness, the stakes are raised when either the audience size or its importance to your speaking success changes. Somehow ancestral memory seems to kick in and you feel out of place: exposed, facing an assembly of human beings whose intentions are unclear. You're painfully aware of being in unfamiliar surroundings among people you may not recognize.

It's a recipe for a dish named SELF-CONSCIOUSNESS. And the only thing that matters is getting out of the exposed (i.e., dangerous) situation as quickly as possible.

In order to remedy this situation—to reduce your self-consciousness and bring your focus back where it needs to be—you have to grapple with a personality trait that's undermining your success.

That trait is *narcissism*.

This isn't to suggest that you're like the media mogul who said a few years ago, "If I only had a little humility, I'd be perfect." It isn't even to say that narcissism in public speaking is a desire on your part to be at the center of things.

Still, that's how it works out if your self-consciousness is at a peak while you're speaking. Let's look at this apparent contradiction and how it plays out in terms of your public speaking fear.

NARCISSISM AND YOU AS A SPEAKER

Just coming to the conclusion I shared above wasn't easy or clear-cut. In fact, I took a chance, some years ago, concerning the people who came to me for help with speech anxiety. I gambled that they wouldn't mind if I told them they were acting like narcissists. That gamble paid off. Since then, discussing narcissism has become an essential tool in my work helping people overcome their fear of public speaking.

This wasn't a great insight on my part. It simply involved listening to what my clients were saying.

As I listened to these people talk about their speech anxiety, it struck me that almost every sentence I was hearing began the same way. You try it. Listen to these stage fright sufferers describe their experiences with speaking fear:

- "I could hear my voice shaking."
- "I thought I was going to go blank and forget my content."
- "I had a panic attack just before I got up to speak."
- "I lay awake for weeks worrying about an upcoming presentation."
- "I could feel the sweat break out as we went around the table introducing ourselves."
- "I wanted to run out of the room."
- "I couldn't see the audience—it was like I suddenly went blind!"

You noticed didn't you that every sentence began with the word "I"?

Where, I wondered, were the words indicating the audience: "they," "them," or "their" . . . or even "we" or "our" to discuss what these speakers and their listeners were experiencing together?

It was suddenly crystal clear to me that the audience members, the most important people in the room, were being left out of the picture entirely by these anxious speakers!

That's when I realized that those who suffer from extreme stage fright are living in a world of narcissism.[28] At the same time, this valuable insight opened up profitable avenues to treat the problem.

I began my solution with the "Two Universes" exercise on the next page.

---

28 Do you know the origin of the term? Narcissus was a beautiful young man in Greek mythology who rejected all who loved him. As punishment, the gods made him fall in love with his own reflection in a forest pool, and he wasted away because he couldn't bear to leave that reflection. According to the myth, the narcissus flower grew up on that spot.

EXERCISE 9-1

THE TWO UNIVERSES

The exercise I created to deal with public speaking narcissism is called the "Two Universes." It's my attempt to make clear to anxious speakers the sheer reality, and consequences, of their self-centered approach to speech performance.

I knew, of course, that people suffering from a speaking phobia don't expect to be told that they're too wrapped up in themselves! Yet, the link seemed so clear that I thought bringing it out in the open would be an important step toward self-awareness and recovery.

Here's the exercise. (Incidentally, I realize that a more accurate name for the visualization would be "The Two Solar Systems." But I couldn't resist the idea that someone is in the wrong universe entirely if they're being narcissistic about public speaking!)

Visualize a children's book image of our solar system. In this version, however, instead of the sun being at the center, there's a star with the word ME visible on its surface. Revolving around this star is *everything else* in the entire universe.

Now imagine you're looking at an illustration of our actual solar system. The sun, the familiar planets, the asteroid belt between Mars and Jupiter, they're all there. Our star, the sun or Sol extends its life-giving radiance to this tiny sector of the Milky Way, the way it always has. And that sustains our beautiful blue-green planet Earth.

Which universe do you occupy when you speak in public?

If you exist in the ME universe, you place yourself at the center of everything. Whatever happens during your presentation, you observe it and analyze it only as it relates to your experience—whether you feel comfortable or uncomfortable, focused or distracted, confident or in panic mode. You become the measure of your success!

That way of thinking is fine if you're an egotist. But if your goal is to influence your audience positively and give them something of value, it's not so "hot" (sorry!).

The universe of successful public speaking demands that the audience be the sun at the center of things, not you. Your audience is the only reason your speech or presentation exists at all, and influencing them positively is the true measure of your success.

Here's the really good news: If you invest yourself in THEM instead of yourself, you will disappear into your message—a reaction that's the exact opposite of narcissism. It's also one of the most helpful outcomes imaginable for reducing speaking self-consciousness.

So, are you in a ME or THEM mode when you speak? If the former, you need to make a 180-degree turn.

PIVOTING 180 DEGREES: THE WAGON SET

Have you ever watched a play where the entire set revolved on a platform, so an entirely new interior or exterior scene slid into place within seconds? That's called a *wagon set*—a common method of changing a scene when there isn't a lot of "fly space" above the stage to raise or lower scenery.

You can use the same concept to turn your thinking around if you've been practicing speech narcissism. Think of it this way: If you're in a narcissistic mode when you speak, it's like your name is appearing above you in marquee theater lights: NOW APPEARING . . . YOU!

But you're not the star of the show[29]—your audience is. So it's time to let your own wagon set revolve to put you exactly opposite where you are now. In swinging around 180 degrees, you're placing your audience at center stage rather than yourself.

Voila! Now it's your listeners who are illuminated by the spotlights, while you're sitting in the house (i.e., auditorium) where it's cool, dark, and comfortable. Your focus at last is where it needs to be: not on yourself but on the people you're there to persuade, move, inspire. They're the main attraction in this show.

Which is exactly how it should be.

---

29 And of course, the more you make yourself the central attraction, the more important it is that you "perform" brilliantly, adding more pressure on yourself.

TOUGH LOVE FOR PUBLIC SPEAKING

You now have a new awareness of the narcissistic component of speech fear, and a visualization to literally "put you in the right place" when you speak to audiences. Let's go one step further concerning how you can become less self-centered in order to feed your own success as a speaker.

First, a mini-review of what you've learned so far in this chapter: You've heard about the link between narcissism and speaking anxiety. You've visualized the Two Universes: one real, one ego-centered. And you've learned about turning your mind around so the audience rather than you is at center stage.

At this point, you're ready for some *tough love* concerning a non-narcissistic approach to speaking in public. If you don't know the term, "tough love" means saying or doing something to someone you care about that may be painful for them, but that is ultimately for their own good. So in that spirit, here are four tough love messages that should help you overcome your extreme self-consciousness while speaking:

1. **Get over Yourself.** You deserve praise for giving speeches and presentations in spite of your nervousness. Still, if you *are* focusing on your mental and physical responses while speaking, you need to realize that you're the least important person in the room. Remember: your audience is at the center of the entire public speaking dynamic. You're there to reach out to them, not to reach inward to yourself.

2. **It Ain't about You.** Hey, what makes you think this audience is here because of *you*? They're contributing their valuable time attending this event because they hope to get something out of it. Instead of being concerned about your own feelings, ask yourself if you're meeting your audience's needs.

3. **People Don't Care about You.** That may sound harsh, but it's true. People are always in a "What's-in-it-for-me?" mode when they attend a talk, lecture, presentation, or speech. They aren't paying any attention to your nervousness or discomfort. And the odds are they don't care about your looks either. They're concerned instead with the informa-

tion they'll receive and whether their time is well spent. All of this is good news for you as the presenter!

4. **Be Professional.** You have a professional responsibility to do your job by giving this speech or presentation. It's what you're being paid for, or at least receiving recognition for. So shut up and do it!

Lecture over. Kindly have the car keys back by 11 p.m.

Love, Dad.

EXERCISE 9-2

EXERCISE FOR MINDFULNESS: YOURSELF

Your ego was just given a few whacks. It's time now for you to rest up and relax a bit.

So here's an exercise that's just as effective in reducing self-consciousness as the other activities in this chapter, but that accomplishes its goal more soothingly. It's the last of the mindfulness exercises from Thich Nhat Hanh that you'll encounter in Fearless Speaking. It's called, paradoxically, "Yourself."

YOURSELF

Sit in a dark room by yourself, or alone by a river at night, or anywhere else where there is solitude. Begin to take hold of your breath. Give rise to the thought, "I will use my finger to point at myself," and then instead of pointing at your body, point away in the opposite direction. Contemplate seeing yourself outside of your bodily form. Contemplate seeing your bodily form present before you—in the trees, the grass and leaves, the river. Be mindful that you are in the universe and the universe is in you: if the universe is, you are; if you are, the universe is. There is no birth. There is no death. There is no coming. There is no going. Maintain the half-smile. Take hold of your breath. Contemplate for 10 to 20 minutes.

EXERCISE 9-3

GETTING COMFORTABLE WITH YOUR BODY

Now you're going to work on a problem that is generally unrecognized as a source of self-consciousness while speaking. Yet this problem adds considerably to the pressure you experience in these situations. I'm talking about the physical exposure you face when appearing in front of others.

Have you ever considered this amazing fact: most of us are perfectly comfortable in our bodies most of the time, yet become acutely self-conscious of them during a speech? More even than the ever-present question, "What do I do with my hands?" we sometimes don't seem to know what to do with any part of ourselves.

The list is long of public speaking mannerisms and postures caused by self-consciousness: wandering, shifting one's weight from one to the other hip, crossing and uncrossing the legs, the "tiger-in-the-cage" pacing syndrome, or "worrying" one's notes. Then there's assuming the fig leaf position or the hands-behind-the-back stance, grasping a lectern with white knuckles, creating a "church steeple" shape with the fingers pressed together at the tips . . . the Spectacle of the Nervous Speaker goes on and on.

Sometimes these mannerisms are so at odds with whatever the speaker is trying to say that it rivets an audience's attention, obliterating everything else. Here are three examples from speakers I've observed:

The Belly-Rubber. A fashionably dressed female executive had a habit, of which she was totally unaware, of rubbing her belly every few minutes as she spoke. There was no logical reason for the action that anyone could determine. When viewing this behavior on videotape, I was told after the event, she was completely horrified. Of course, her audience members soon lost interest in whatever she was saying—they were just waiting for the next belly rub!

The Lectern Abuser. Another speaker's modus operandi was to regularly stroll away from the lectern, then wander back and kick it! It wasn't a hard kick, and he appeared to do it absentmindedly. But I'm sure audience members beside myself were wondering what the poor lectern had ever done to him to deserve this physical abuse.

The Incredible Folding Man. Just before beginning his speech, this gentleman placed his feet closely together and then began to fold himself up. He clasped his hands tightly, with his chin resting on his thumbs, and somehow reduced his corporeal presence by about half—right there in front of us listening to his business presentation. It was like watching a magician perform a slow-motion vanishing trick!

Imagine for a moment that you're an audience member watching any of these individuals speak. Would you be able to focus on what was being said when each presenter was offering such an entertaining mime show?

Each of these speakers was experiencing—and expressing physically—a terrible sense of being exposed. Their bodies probably seemed suddenly superfluous, perhaps even to be their enemy.

Let's look at how you can avoid this dilemma in your own speeches. After all, you need your body to be your ally rather than a source of acute self-consciousness.

THE DUCK-AND-WATER VISUALIZATION

If you recall from the "Grounding" and "Suiting the Action to the Word" exercises in Chapter Four, the most natural position for you when you speak is standing upright with your hands hanging straight down at your sides. Now, let's take this a step further. If you stand this way, bringing your hands up only when they're needed, they won't get in the way and make you (or your audience) aware of them. When you really need to make a gesture, i.e., when you can't not use your hands any longer, make that gesture. At that moment, the gesture will not only be unavoidable, but a natural consequence of the point you're trying to make. It will therefore support and amplify your content, as a gesture should.

Now, I understand that standing with your hands hanging down by your sides takes some getting used to. It feels awkward at first—even though it looks perfectly natural to your audience. To get yourself comfortable with this "neutral" posture, you can use the duck-and-water visualization, which is this: Imagine that you're a duck standing up tall with your wings at your sides. Since you've most likely just waddled out of a lake or pond, water is running down your wings (arms) and dripping from the ends of your speculum (fingers).

Plunk.

Plunk.

Plunk.

And that's it. It's a pretty simple visualization, and one that's certainly easy to achieve.

Practice this, and you'll get in the habit of keeping your arms and hands at your sides when you speak, ready to be brought into action only when you need them. No more flapping your wings . . . sorry, arms[30] around inappropriately, like a duck out of water.

Yes, this particular visualization is a bit silly. But it can be effective in helping you eliminate a major cause of your self-consciousness while speaking: the feeling that you don't know what to do with your hands.

AN EXERCISE FOR BEING MORE COMFORTABLE IN FRONT OF OTHERS

By now you should have accepted the idea that you don't have to DO anything physically when presenting, except to respond naturally to your message as you deliver it to your audience. Let's go one step further to get you more relaxed at being "exposed" in front of groups.

I put that word in quotation marks, because when you stand in front of others to speak, it's really not very different from the kind of speaking you do every day. Whichever situation you find yourself in, it's still you talking about things that interest you. You should be comfortable being that person in front of any audience, from one person to much larger gatherings.

Here's an exercise for GETTING YOU MORE COMFORTABLE WITH EXPOSURE:

---

30 Couldn't resist that one!

1. Stand and imagine you're in front of a good-sized audience. Close your eyes.

2. Smile.

3. Open your eyes. Keep smiling.

That's it.

What you can keep in mind is that taking a physical stance or assuming a facial expression can create an emotional response on its own. We all know that emotions bring about physical responses: tears start to flow when you're sad; when you're happy you smile, etc. But it also works in the opposite direction: take on a hangdog expression and you'll feel sad, stand with your hands on your hips and you'll feel more powerful. So the smile you just practiced reminds you that being in front of others can actually be an enjoyable experience. After all, you already do it every day of your life.

EXERCISE 9-4

6 MORE WAYS TO REDUCE NERVOUSNESS

As a last point in this chapter's focus on reducing self-consciousness and nervousness when you speak, here are six additional tips:

- **Acquire speaking experience.** We always fear the unknown, and the more frequently you speak, the more natural an activity it will seem for you.

- **Prepare! Prepare! Prepare!** Rehearse three to five times. Go through your presentation enough times that the talking points come to you readily, but not so many times that you become mechanical. Practice in the real setting with the real equipment wherever possible.

- **Think positively.** You're far and away the person best positioned to beat up on yourself. But why do that? Spend your preparation and "pondering" time prior to a presentation thinking positively, so you can create a self-fulfilling prophecy of success.

- **Remember that most nervousness is not visible.** It's only you who are "inside" this nervous speaker. Your audience is interested in what you have to tell them. They're not focused on your nervousness because they probably don't see it.

- **Be at your best physically and mentally.** Get rest and give yourself quiet time if you need it (if you're an introvert), or mix-and-mingle to get your juices flowing (if you're an extrovert).

- **Don't expect prefection!**[31] Your audiences expect you to be good, not perfect.

---

31 Oops! Guess I'm not *prefect!*

SEAN

When Sean completed the Stage Fright quiz in our first session, he scored in the "high level of stage fright" category. Sean is an executive chef in the hospitality industry, overseeing a prominent brand of hotels. He gives two types of presentations frequently: formal "discussions" to upper management and more informal "tossed-together-the-day-before" (as he put it) talks to chefs and restaurant staff of the hotels.

You can guess which type of speaking he was comfortable with and which made him anxious. His high-anxiety categories, in fact, applied almost exclusively to his presentations to higher-ups. When giving these talks to senior management, he experienced some nervousness beforehand, but his level of anxiety *while speaking* was off the charts.

Sean felt that he was simply out of place in front of the VIPs. He used a variety of metaphors to explain his own self-image: "fish out of water," "imposter," "out of my league," and so on. The truth was, these presentations shouldn't have been inherently stressful. The CEO and other senior execs were experts on financial matters and didn't understand Sean's area of expertise at all!

They were looking for assurances that Sean had a clear vision for the operation of the hotel restaurants and a firm hand in implementing that vision. They weren't judging him, and they certainly didn't care a bit whether he was a charismatic speaker. Once we were able to point his thinking in the right direction, i.e., at his talking points rather than his "performance," he became a much more focused and less self-conscious speaker.

10

BIOFEEDBACK FOR PHYSICAL SYMPTOMS AND PANIC ATTACKS

Like the previous pages in *Fearless Speaking*, this chapter is concerned with relieving your speech anxiety during your speeches and presentations. In particular, however, the focus of this chapter is on the *physiological* responses that accompany your speaking fear.

Before getting to this essential approach to controlling stage fright, let's review your progress up to this point.

You've now put your fear of public speaking into perspective and learned how to restructure your negative thinking (Chapters One and Two). You've worked on proper breathing techniques to establish greater self-control (Chapter Three). You've learned the tools for improving your physical presence (Chapter Four), along with ways to stay fully focused and to connect with audiences (Chapters Five and Six). You've worked on your vocal expressiveness (Chapter Seven), and practiced visualization techniques for positive outcomes when you speak (Chapter Eight). In Chapter Nine, you raised your awareness concerning how to overcome feelings of self-consciousness and exposure while speaking.

Now it's time to work on increasing your sense of *control* as a presenter. You do this by learning how to regulate your body's responses to the "fearful" speaking event.

That's because as well armed as you now are concerning approaches to overcoming speaking fear, you still have to deal with how your body responds when you get up in front of an audience. You might say that while your brain now gets it, your body still isn't convinced that public speaking is a safe activity.

To put this another way: however well you deal with the psychology and emotional aspects of speaking fear, you can't think your way through the physiology of your body's responses. The way to deal with what's happening to you physically is to turn those responses to your advantage. That's what we'll be looking at in this chapter.

GETTING YOURSELF READY FOR ACTION

Whatever else public speaking represents for you, it's literally an *exciting* activity. Your body becomes energized and ready for action. Your job is to *harness* that energy into constructive channels so you can be relaxed yet dynamic rather than at the mercy of undirected and even chaotic impulses.

To do so, you first need to gain a greater awareness of your physical reaction, and then learn how to use *biofeedback* to monitor your progress. By succeeding in these twin goals, you will:

- Slow down and quiet your stress response.
- "Close the gate" through which stressful stimuli reach your awareness.
- Increase helpful blood flow during times of stress.
- Open your "emotional gate" for a positive performance and greater confidence.
- Create a distraction trigger to center and calm you physically before speaking.

THE PHYSIOLOGY OF SPEAKING FEAR

Let's take a look at how the human body responds to public speaking anxiety.

What to some people would simply be "butterflies," is to those with severe speaking anxiety a *fearful* event, invoking the need to fight or flee the danger. That's the well known "fight-or-flight response". Since neither of those actions is possible when giving a presentation, your strong physical reactions and sense of "being trapped" can be acute. And of course, an additional difficulty is that you must cope with these extreme physical responses *while giving your speech*!

Your body's fearful reactions to speech anxiety usually include some of the following physical symptoms:

- Rapid, shallow breathing
- Increased heart rate
- Rise in blood pressure
- Release of the stress hormone epinephrine, also known as adrenaline
- Release of cortisol (another, less well-known stress hormone. See below.)
- Sweating
- Dry mouth
- Cold extremities as blood retreats to vital organs and blood vessels constrict
- Cessation of digestion and peristalsis (movement of food through the bowels)

In addition, you can experience any of these physiological reactions as well:

- Pounding heart
- Becoming pale or flushed
- Shaky voice
- Trembling hands or legs
- Loss of hearing

- Tunnel vision or not being able to see the audience
- Mind becoming "cobwebby" or in a fog

Obviously, fear of public speaking can produce extreme physiological responses! Reactions like those above can negatively affect your entire performance.

This tendency of your body to respond so strongly to speech anxiety is the reason why the mind-based approach we've looked at so far—including cognitive restructuring, positive visualization, and increased focus and presence—isn't enough. You must control your pronounced physical responses as well in order to be effective in the speaking situation.[32]

THE DANGERS OF CORTISOL

One of those physical reactions is the release of the stress hormone *cortisol*. Cortisol is a naturally occurring hormone produced by the adrenal glands. The beneficial effects of this substance include the following functions:

- Processing of glucose level in the body
- Regulating blood pressure
- Production of insulin to control blood sugar
- A healthy immune system
- Controlling inflammation

However, *prolonged high levels* of stress-related cortisol in the bloodstream—such as in longstanding speech anxiety and stage fright—have been shown to have harmful effects on the body. These include:

- Decreased cognitive abilities
- Suppression of thyroid function
- High blood sugar
- Impairment of bone density
- Reduction in muscle tissue

---

32   One chapter of *Fearless Speaking* has covered, in part, an area based in physiological response: Chapter Three, "Breathing Techniques for Relaxation and Control."

- Increased blood pressure
- Reduced immune system function and response to inflammation
- Abdominal fat deposits, which are associated with health problems such as heart attack and strokes[33]

Clearly, using biofeedback to counter such a public speaking-related stress response is important to your physical well-being. To examine how to do so, let's start at the very source of the physiologically based response to public speaking: your awareness that you're giving a performance. One organ in particular responds immediately and strongly to that news.

THE HEART OF THE MATTER

You may or may not believe that the heart is the seat of the emotions, but there's no denying that this organ plays a starring role in your response to *glossophobia* and your awareness of how your body reacts when you speak in public.

It may interest you to know, for instance, that if you experience fear of public speaking, you probably have a higher heart rate than someone with a more generalized social anxiety disorder.[34] Literally, then, public speaking fear is not just "in your head."

When your pulse rate begins to gallop, when your heart pounds so that it feels like it's going to break out of your chest, when the engine of your circulatory system is startled out of its normal rhythm, you can't escape the fact that the situation is out of your control. You want to establish equilibrium again quickly. In fact, you desperately need to do so if you're going to present a calm, confident, and professional demeanor.

This, then, is where you need to start in terms of biofeedback: calming your heart so the rest of your body and your mind can follow.

---

33 http://stress.about.com/od/stresshealth/a/cortisol.htm. Accessed February 19, 2011.

34 Hofmann and Otto, *Cognitive Behavioral Therapy*, 10.

EXERCISE 10-1

CALMING THE HEART

You'll begin by becoming acquainted with your own "normal state": the starting point you can return to in times of stress.

To do so, first determine your resting pulse. That's the number of beats per minute when you're not under stress or in physical exertion. Count your pulse rate for ten seconds and multiply by six; or continue taking your pulse for a full minute. Make a mental note of that number. Now continue feeling your pulse as you . . .

. . . take a DEEP breath and hold it for a slow count of five. Then release that big breath all at once: WHOOSH!

Did you just notice any change in your pulse rate?

You may have felt your heart slow down briefly just after you whooshed out the breath. That's because when you breathe deeply, a full reservoir of air moves from your lungs to your heart where it is pumped into the bloodstream oxygenating the cells throughout your body. Since your heart has just received a generous supply of oxygen, it doesn't have to work as hard.

Oxygen means life, and when the heart is fully oxygenated, it can slow down and not "try as hard." The other important effect produced here, is that the sheer controlled slowness of the breathing process counteracts the rapid heartbeat that accompanies your fear response. In a sense, your heart can take it easy again because you're giving it permission to do so.

This is an important physiological response for you to learn in order to work against the loss of control that comes with speaking anxiety. By inducing your heart to slow down and relax, you're countering one of the most noticeable and worrying effects of stage fright: the sensation that your body is working against you.

This simple exercise is a way to reestablish control and to create a positive rather than negative physiological response to speaking in public. It also helps directly link breathing and heart rate, demonstrating that control of this process is possible.

Practice it some more now: Monitor your pulse rate, breathe deeply, and link the two. The more you can use slow controlled breathing in anxiety-inducing situations, the more you will be able to calm yourself and handle those events.

Nicely done! You've just started using biofeedback to reduce your stress response to public speaking.

EXERCISE 10-2

CLOSING THE STRESS GATE

You've now learned something about how the mind-to-body chan-nel works in perceiving and responding to stress. You may have heard of this process compared to a "gate," especially with regard to controlling pain. Visualizing keeping the gate closed, for in-stance, can diminish the amount of pain signals—or at least the awareness of them—that reaches the consciousness.

Methods of "closing" the gate include simply being distracted, relaxation exercises, meditation, and intense focus on a task. In times of emergency or danger, such as in a battle or car accident, people have performed amazing feats despite injuries that should have been accompanied by intense pain. In fact, they report that they were unaware of any pain at the time.[35]

Learning that it's possible to control pain or manage an exces-sive physical response to stress is enormously helpful. In Chap-ter Two of this book ("Changing Your Negative Thinking"), you practiced reshaping your cognitive responses to public speaking fear. Now you can work on the physiological changes that take place when you speak.

Exercise 10-1 above involved calming the heart. In the following Exercise 10-2, "Closing the Stress Gate," you'll visualize disrupting the messages from your body to your brain that keep reminding you of your fear. In effect, you'll be closing the gate to an unpro-ductive part of your consciousness.

The important question here is: What closes the gate for you? If you already have an effective distraction,[36] a relaxation exercise, a meditation technique or other trigger that draws your attention, you may already know how to effectively close the gate. If not, I would like to offer a visualization that may work for you:

Focus on making the various areas in your awareness a single area.

---

35 "Use the Gate Control Model to Manage Pain," handout from Brigham and Women's Hospital Pain Management Center.

36 One of my clients, a nurse, particularly liked the idea of a distraction to take her mind off her fear just before she spoke in public. She understood perfectly how this would help her, since she'd already used the technique for years with patients who feared needles: she would say something to distract them just before she inserted the needle in their arm.

That is, close the gate to the noisy mob of distractions trying to bully its way into your consciousness. There are too many things that are pulling your focus away from where it needs to be. You are multitasking—a completely counterproductive habit in public speaking, when 100% focus on a single outcome is needed. Some of those tasks, in fact, involve caring for and feeding your anxiety, which you should certainly stop doing. You have four or five balls in the air at one time. No wonder your fears and inadequacies are crowding your mind!

Let all of these things go, allowing yourself the luxury of focusing on the one area that truly matters to you at this moment: Your audience and the message you have to give them.

Now, the visualization itself:

As you prepare to speak, see yourself stepping through an actual gate leading to your performance area. Now immediately latch the gate (before that crowd of worries can follow you).

The gate is now officially closed behind you.

In *front* of you are the people you're here to talk to. You and they are the only ones in this space. It's peaceful and cozy here. Outside the gate the winds of discord are blowing, but the sound is far away and you can no longer hear it.

EXERCISE 10-3

OPENING THE EMOTIONAL GATE

As important as it is to close the gate against fear-induced think-ing that will alter your behavior, it's vital to open the emotional barrier you've erected against your listeners. You may not realize that this has been occurring, but the chances are good that it has. After all, if you have speaking anxiety audiences seem dangerous. Without them sitting out there waiting for you to prove yourself, why would there be a problem?

What this means in terms of your performance is that in order to gain protection you may be hiding your true self from view. But to fully overcome the negative physical responses that you're experi-encing, you have to emerge from this fine and private hiding place.

That's because an "emotional gate" that's latched shut sends your body the wrong signals as to how it should respond. Your emotional make-up and your physiological responses are close-ly linked, after all. Appropriate emotions for speaking in public include joy, fun, and an eagerness to share what you know—not dread, aversion, and a grim determination to survive the torture that's about to occur. Think of the nonverbal cues you exhibit when you experience the latter set of emotions!

As I've said elsewhere in this book: nervousness about public speaking is normal and healthy; anxiety is not. If you retreat emotionally from your audience, it will only prolong the pain and leave you more vulnerable.

So at this point I want to talk about opening the emotional gate so you can be both strong and vulnerable for your audience. People who show their vulnerability make audiences want to reach out to them. Those who wear armor or bare their teeth at listeners send them in the opposite direction.

Learning to Accept Your Environment. Consider the shiver response. It's normal to shiver when you're cold, because your body is trying to generate heat through movement in the muscles. Eventually, though, constant shivering just reminds you that you're cold, and the cycle keeps repeating. I discovered during the Massachusetts winters when I was growing up that if I consciously stopped the shivering—if I willed myself to remain still—I didn't feel as cold! In a way, I was accepting the low temperatures and telling myself to just remain calm in the face of them.

In other words, I was accepting my environment rather than trying to escape from it. Can you see how doing the same thing in front of an audience will keep you physically calm and still, rather than tight and "shivering"?

Acupuncture provides another example. Acupuncturists believe that the body's energy or qi (pronounced "chee") has been blocked somewhere. The acupuncture needles penetrate these blockages, helping release your body's energy along the "meridians" through which the qi flows. Once your qi is flowing freely again, pain and other negative effects of blocked energy are lessened.

Frightened and anxious speakers block their emotions in similar fashion. The essential interaction between speaker and audience can't then take place, because one side (the speaker) is shutting down its signal. To be in the spotlight in front of a group when this is happening—when no real communication is taking place—is to virtually guarantee that you'll be miserable on stage. And if you feel unhappy, you will reflect it physically. That's the negative biofeedback loop that ties emotional unhappiness with physical discomfort in public speaking.

Remember, audiences won't remember the facts and figures you throw at them as much as they will recall how you made them feel. Of course, the process also works in the opposite direction: you will remember particular audiences by your emotional response to them and the speaking situation more strongly than, say, the questions they asked.

"Avoiding Excellence." But blocking your own emotions is only part of your unhappiness as an anxious speaker. Another element of the hurdle you're erecting for yourself comes from your desire to be "excellent." In fact, one of the greatest fallacies of giving presentations is that you have to be an excellent public speaker.

The truth is you only have to be an honest speaker. If you know what you're talking about and are passionate about sharing it with others, you'll come across as natural and interesting. And *if you don't have the necessary knowledge, expertise, or genuine concern for your listeners, trying to "be excellent" won't get you there.*

The surest path to excellence in public speaking is not to aim for that ideal but to aim for honesty. Audiences want to hear you, not you-trying-to-be-a-better-speaker-than-you-really-are.

When you get used to that idea—when you can stand in front of a group of people honestly and give them only what you're capable of—you'll be taking a huge weight off your shoulders. After all, what's easier, being you or being excellent?

When you speak as yourself rather than as an ideal, something infinitely valuable will emerge: true communication. Open the emotional gate and welcome your audience in. Let them see your vulnerability rather than being terrified of it. The flow of communication will then occur.

EXERCISE 10-4

FACIAL RELAXATION

It's a genuine not-seeing-the-forest-for-the-trees situation: your face is helping generate your own negative biofeedback. Facial expressiveness or countenance is an area many people ignore when thinking about nonverbal communication. Yet your face is not only highly flexible, it's an essential tool for getting your message and meaning across.

Consider for a moment how visually dependent we humans are. We use facial structures and features to recognize one person from another. And we read subtle signs of intention and meaning by the sometimes finely tuned expressions we see on another person's face. Obviously, if you're a stone-faced speaker, you're putting yourself and your audience at a disadvantage!

Because the face is physical like some of your other nonverbal communication tools, it can become tight and unresponsive when you're stressed. It's made up of muscles after all. A common place for holding tension, for instance, is the area around the eyes.

Clearly, it's helpful for you to practice relaxing your facial muscles so they can remain pliant enough for full expressiveness. Along those lines, try these facial relaxation exercises:

> Allow your face to go completely slack. You might not want to look in a mirror while doing this, as your muscle tone will not be especially flattering. Pay particular attention to your eye sockets. Feel the tension you hold in this "secret" spot. Now let it melt away.

> You should be experiencing a feeling of calmness and a sense of being in the present moment. Now tighten your face—not radically, but just enough so that you can sense how you may hold tension in your face without even realizing it. Imagine how that tension can subtly drain your energy all day long.

> Go completely slack again, and hold that facial posture. Now allow your personality to flow back into your features. This

is you at your best: the image of calm attentiveness, without any tension.

Use your muscle memory to retain how your face feels when it's like this: alive with your personality, minus tension. It's one more biofeedback channel through which you can send yourself messages that get you to the right place physically. And you'll be helping to keep those wrinkles away too!

EXERCISE 10-5

THE HEALING BREATH

The Healing Breath is an original approach I use in my work. It's a way to help liberate yourself from negative feelings, as you relax your nervous system through inward-directed breathing and awareness.

Remember in Chapter Five when you practiced the Focused Relaxation exercise?[37] You became aware of thoughts that arose in your mind but you didn't invest yourself in them. You noticed but didn't engage those thoughts nor did you actively resist them. In a similar way, The Healing Breath helps you recognize unhelpful emotions without perpetuating them. By practicing The Healing Breath, you allow your body to respond physically to healthy breathing, so the signals you receive are positive and affirming:

1. *Sit quietly, relaxing your facial muscles and your eyes. Allow any negative energy to become heavy and sink downward, like sediment in a pond. Don't disturb this energy, just let it settle down and be still.*

2. *Now with your eyes closed, visualize yourself smiling. Don't actually smile; just visualize yourself doing it. First your face will relax . . . and then, without consciously activating the muscles, you'll genuinely smile. (Smiles are infectious,[38] even to ourselves!) Remember that a smile begins at the corner of the eyes, not at the mouth.*

3. *While still smiling, follow your breath with your consciousness. Both your smile and your breathing are easy and delicious. If your face feels in any way tight from smiling, change the smile to a grin, and keep it going. (A grin can make the "crinkly" feeling at the corner of your eyes even more noticeable.)*

---

37 See Exercise 5-1, "Focused Relaxation."

38 Speaking of "infectious" facial movements: Did you know that dogs will yawn as easily as we do when they see a yawn, and that they'll yawn much more easily when their *owner* yawns? It's true!

4. Scan yourself inwardly. Any anger present? Any impatience or frustration? Any fearfulness? If so, turn your "smile-breath" on each of these emotions until the negative energy residing there melts, sinking downward in that pond.

5. Now expand your breathing, letting it reach every nook and cranny in your body. Send your breath into every space and organ of your physical presence. Your breath is a healing solution. Allow it to flow and fill you everywhere.

EXERCISE 10-6

STRATEGIES FOR PANIC ATTACKS

Finally in this chapter, I'd like to discuss ways you can help yourself if you experience a panic attack during a presentation. We'll be looking at three such "escape hatches."

You may need one of these escape hatches if despite your best intentions and the techniques you've learned from this book, you feel a powerful and overwhelming need to flee the speaking situation.

The suggestions in the general literature concerning this problem are remarkably unhelpful. Here are some actual strategies offered by "experts" and lay persons for dealing with public speaking-induced panic attacks:

- *Speak to people's foreheads*
- *Look at specific points in the room and talk to those areas*
- *Take deep breaths before speaking*
- *Pray*
- *Talk to someone about it*
- *Remember that it is a curable condition*
- *Contact a medical professional and seek guidance*
- *Realize you didn't die from the attack—then you'll be able to laugh about it!*
- *Build your confidence back to where it used to be*
- *Don't fear fear*
- *React with confidence at the instant you feel the anxiety attack*
- *Push your energy outward, not back into your body*
- *Practice*
- *Take a tranquilizer*
- *Tell yourself you can do this, so stop panicking!*
- *Accept the fact that public speaking is not inherently stressful*

- Relinquish your need to control your environment
- Eat foods with life in them (!)
- Distract yourself
- Eliminate anxious thoughts

And the perennial favorite:

- Imagine the audience naked or in their underwear

Can you figure out how any of these techniques will stop a panic attack in its tracks? I can't!

Look at those approaches again. You'll notice that not a single one discusses the essential task of the speaker suffering a panic attack, i.e., the need to deal with the situation that's actually taking place!

The three solutions I offer below ("Escape Hatches 1, 2, and 3") all work by doing just that: allowing you to face the situation and handle it rather than giving in to the panic. They place you securely in the room and help you deal productively with the situation at hand.

The reason I've formulated these particular approaches is because I believe public speaking-related panic attacks always arise from the same cause: a speaker who feels divorced from his or her audience. The audience may be viewed as hostile, bored, uncaring, or judgmental. But in every instance, the speaker feels that the audience is there, and he or she is here, across a psychological divide. And "here" always seems like a lonely and dangerous place. No wonder, then, that that presenter feels like Jonathan Harker in Dracula who says woefully, "There is no escape for me!"

> *I believe public speaking-related panic attacks always arise from the same cause: a speaker who feels divorced from his or her audience.*

In fact, there is no literal escape when a panic attack hits you during a speech or presentation. You can't run screaming from the room (unless you don't actually enjoy your job any more).

And you can't stop the presses and say, "Sorry everybody, I simply can't go on." Just as in life, the only way out is through—and the time to deal with the situation is "now."

How to Stop a Panic Attack. To stop a panic attack in a public speaking situation, you must eliminate the cause of the panic, which is your divorce from your audience. When you can bring yourself back to the here-and-now—of you talking to these people on a topic of mutual interest—you will share with your listeners something valuable and irreplaceable: this moment in time, in this place.

And that is an invitation to excitement and enjoyment, not fear.

So, the three escape hatches I've crafted to help you during a panic attack:

ESCAPE HATCH #1: THE ONLY WAY OUT IS THROUGH

Follow these four steps, in this sequence, for handling a panic attack that occurs during your speech or presentation:

1. STOP whatever it is you are saying, doing, or thinking.

2. Breathe deeply, once.

3. Bring yourself back into mindfulness. Inhabit the present moment again, fully, without being (or wishing you were) someplace else. Look at the people there with you.

4. Resume talking about whatever it is that matters to them, NOT you. If you weren't doing that before, do it now!

If you're concerned that the moment when you stop and take a deep breath will be too noticeable, use body language to make it look as if you're gathering your thoughts. Or take a drink of water after you breathe deeply. Use your wits!

The key to this escape hatch is that, when you give yourself over to the needs of others, your self-consciousness about yourself disappears. Notice that Step 4 says, "Talk about what matters to them." As soon as you do, you'll realize that you're in the right place, with the right listeners, discussing something that you're all interested in. After all, it's not about you—it's about what you need to tell them and what they need to hear. Get on that wavelength and you'll realize you belong here with them, and they with you.

It's all a reminder that in the end dealing with reality is so much more effective than running from it. And that honesty trumps showmanship every time.

ESCAPE HATCH #2: MOVEMENT WILL SET YOU FREE

Have you heard of the theory of embodied cognition? It states that we think not only with our brain, but also with our body. If you consider this for a moment, it makes perfect sense. Haven't you paced back and forth while trying to remember something? Don't ideas pop into your head when you're driving? When you're scribbling notes for an idea, don't you often think of something else you should be writing down? And doesn't taking a walk usually clear your head and realign your thinking?

The common element in each of these examples is movement. Embodied cognition goes even further, theorizing that we can actually use movement to help us think more productively.

In fact, experiments have demonstrated this benefit. As a recent newspaper article reported:

> A series of studies [showed] that children can solve math problems better if they are told to use their hands while thinking. Another recent study suggested that stage actors remember their lines better when they are moving. And in one study published last year, subjects asked to move their eyes in a specific pattern while puzzling through a brainteaser were twice as likely to solve it.[39]

It stands to reason, then, that movement can help you think at one of the moments when you desperately need to do so: during a public speaking panic attack. So if you find yourself in the speaking pressure-cooker with your agitation building and the thought that you won't remember what to say next . . .

Move!

Cross the room to point to something on the slide screen. Visit a section of the audience you haven't been to in a while. Step back to the lectern if you've been standing somewhere else on the stage, or move away from it if you've been stuck behind the

---

39   Drake Bennett, "Don't Just Stand There, Think," *Boston Globe*, January 13, 2008.

thing for some time. Take a few steps toward another part of the room as you make your next point. It doesn't really matter what you do, just move!

Embodied cognition is telling you that simply by moving, you'll think more clearly and help bring yourself out of the panic. Moving in any way will help you feel less trapped. Also, the nervous energy building in your muscles from adrenaline needs a release, and movement will help provide it.

So use the outlet of movement before you overload.

ESCAPE HATCH #3: INHABITING YOUR BODY

As I mentioned earlier in this section, a primary cause of a spiraling panic attack is the desire to escape the presence of your audience. In a sense, you want to be anywhere but here, dealing with the present situation. But you must deal with it! Longing to be anywhere else in the universe may be momentarily comforting, but it keeps you worlds away from being present and engaged with your listeners.

When your mind is seducing you into panic like this, it's time to get physical.

By all means, stay engaged with your audience mentally and emotionally. But now start paying attention to your body as well.

First, ground yourself. Feel the soles of your feet on the floor and the firm foundation that gives you. Imagine you have roots that go down into the earth, reaching deep and wide so you're steadfast and secure.

Second, feel your breath energizing you. Imagine that your breathing is electric. When you inhale, you're a cylinder of pure power, lit up like a neon sign!

Third, become aware of the physical sensations inside you. Where is the tension? The energy flow? The power? The heat? The miracle of life is coursing through you, giving you strength and animating you. To notice what's going on in your body is to be completely present, to absolutely occupy the here-and-now.

Becoming aware of your body in this way—inhabiting it—is a potent antidote to the fear-induced need to escape your circumstances. You don't need a place of refuge at this moment. You're *right where you need to be, mentally, yes, but also as a body that's occupying an enjoyable moment in time.*

AIDA

Aida is the VP of HR at a company that provides mental health services for state and federal agencies. Her job entails constant travel around the country to "whip everybody into shape" and "put out fires." In fact, she calls herself Chief Firefighter. But despite her jokes, she's a soft-spoken professional who's completely dedicated to the company and its clients.

She came to me because she had an uncommon problem: while speaking to her teams, she would become physically ill. She suffered from "Imposter Syndrome," believing that others would find out eventually that she was unqualified. Her distress made her feel like vomiting and experience what she called "oxygen deprivation," leaving her gasping for air. Aida believed her fear stemmed from when she was 12 years old and had to recite a poem in class. She did poorly, was berated by the teacher, and was scarred by the experience.

I worked with her on some of the biofeedback techniques in this chapter to help her gain control. The concept of measured breathing, for instance, was new to her, and given her hectic schedule, she saw its value immediately. Gradually, she gained control of her respiration so she didn't forget to breathe. She found the technique so helpful in fact that I assigned a diaphragmatic breathing exercise to use in the minutes before she spoke. We also worked on facial relaxation to eliminate a habitual frown.

Aida eventually was able to be fully present and comfortable in the moment (see "Escape Hatch #1" above). She was able to focus on getting her message across without trying to get through it all as quickly as possible . . . before the imposter was found out!

11

SETTING AND ACHIEVING YOUR GOALS

You're almost there!

At this point in *Fearless Speaking*, it's time to take stock of the new tools and approaches you've acquired throughout the book. After that, it's just a question of putting your improved skills to work to achieve greater success in public speaking.

You've probably realized by now that overcoming speaking anxiety is only one step toward becoming an effective speaker. The techniques and practice exercises you've learned from this book will help launch you into an exciting new world where enjoyment and increased influence replace a dread of public speaking in your mind.

But there's more to being a successful speaker than that. Being clear on your goals and your purpose are equally important. Those elements of public speaking, along with a checklist to measure your progress, are what you'll find in this chapter.

EXERCISE 11-1

YOUR PUBLIC SPEAKING TOOLKIT

Consider how far you've come from the person who started reading this guide to more confident speaking! As I'm sure you realize, nothing provides more confidence than the belief that you have the skills and knowledge to succeed. By using the practical approaches in these pages, you can remove the obstacles and roadblocks you've set up against yourself. At the same time, your expertise, passion, and commitment to the topics you talk about will begin to come through more clearly to your listeners.

As you reflect on the things you've learned so far, ask yourself these questions:

1. Which of the many techniques and exercises in these pages resonate most strongly with you?

2. Which make the most sense?

3. Which have proven to be effortless and effective for you as you've tried them?

Your answers to these questions will tell you which techniques work most effectively for you, which you should continue to practice. As you've heard me say before, everyone's experience of stage fright is different. Some techniques will speak to you and others won't, and that's how it should be as you move toward your individual goals as a communicator.

Remind yourself of the exercises now from the list below, which also includes the chapters where you'll find each activity. Then in the space that follows, jot down any of the activities that you found most productive. These exercises are your touchstones for conquering public speaking fear. They are your primary tools for more effective talks, presentations, lectures, business meetings, sales pitches, formal speeches, and every other form of oral communication.

FEARLESS SPEAKING EXERCISES

Do You Have Stage Fright? A Quiz

Chapter 1: Understanding Your Fear of Public Speaking
1-1 Overcoming Speaking Anxiety Will Change Your Life
1-2 Your Public Speaking Strengths
1-3 Talking about Your Strengths
1-4 Understanding Speaking Fear
1-5 Types of Fear Reduction Techniques

Chapter 2: Changing Your Negative Thinking
2-1 Overcoming Worst-Case Thinking
2-2 Developing Positive Coping Statements
2-3 Channeling Your Thinking – The 10s Exercise
2-4 Define Your Objective!

Chapter 3: Breathing Techniques for Relaxation and Control
3-1 Progressive Relaxation
3-2 Mini-Vacation
3-3 Diaphragmatic Breathing

Chapter 4: Body Language to Look and Feel More Confident
4-1 Grounding
4-2 Entering a Room
4-3 Suiting Action to Word: Using the Right Gestures
4-4 Videotaping Your Performance
4-5 Checklists for Body Language and Use of Space

Chapter 5: Staying Focused, Mindful, and on Message
5-1 Focused Relaxation
5-2 Exercises for Mindfulness
5-3 10 Ways to Stay Focused and Present While Speaking

Chapter 6: Connecting with Audiences and Gaining Influence
6-1 Greeting Your Audience
6-2 Using a Grabber
6-3 Creating a Clincher

TOOLKIT: THE BEST EXERCISES AND APPROACHES FOR ME

_____

_____

_____

_____

_____

_____

_____

_____

YOUR DESTINATION IS NOT OVERCOMING ANXIETY

By this point in your efforts at self-improvement, your level of anxiety should no longer be the measuring stick of your success as a speaker. Always keep in mind: your goal is not to reduce your fear. If it is, you're still too focused on your anxiety. Go back to Chapter One on putting your fear into perspective and Chapter Two on cognitive restructuring to go from negative to positive thinking.

Your job is to speak successfully! When you keep your eye on the prize of achieving a beneficial influence with audiences, your anxiety will become sidelined. It will be starved of oxygen as soon as you're focused instead on your action goals. Here's a simple yet profound message that you should remember:

> *Always keep in mind: your goal is not to reduce your fear. If it is, you're still too focused on your anxiety.*

The more you forget yourself, the more you will find yourself as a speaker.

Understand Your Audience to Influence Them. A natural step for you in achieving such success is learning how to analyze your audience. You need to determine your audience's needs so you can develop a way to meet those needs.

Now at last you're traveling beyond the world of your personal fear of public speaking and entering the universe of true speaking influence.

EXERCISE 11-2

PERFORMING AN AUDIENCE ANALYSIS

What's your first thought upon hearing that you'll be giving a presentation?

Is it: "What will my topic be?"

If it is, you're in good company. Most people think along those lines when they know they're going to be speaking in public.

But there's a much more important question you should ask yourself first: not "What is my topic?" but "To whom am I speaking?" For until you know as closely as possible the make-up of your audience, how do you know what to say to them?

In my profession, for instance, there are at least 100 speeches I could give on performing well as a communicator. Each talk would depend upon the age, level of knowledge, sophistication, demographics, and profession of my listeners (among other factors), and how they will use the information I give them. In other words, I need to know whom that audience really is and what they need to hear. I'm sure it's the same in your area of expertise.

Ask yourself what your listeners need to hear (it's not always what they think they need to hear!). Some audiences have a deep level of knowledge and experience, others less so. Do these listeners have preferences concerning how they like to receive information? What are their likes and dislikes that constitute their comfort zone? What are their expectations concerning your presentation?

Once you know these things, you might ask yourself whether you want to meet those expectations or intentionally disregard them. (I think of that last approach as following the advice in Shakespeare's Macbeth to "Be bloody, bold and resolute!")

It may be obvious to you by now that your first step toward achieving your goals is understanding with whom you're dealing. Yet speakers too often leap onto the information-delivery bandwagon without a moment's thought concerning the true nature of their audience. These speakers are armed and ready to fire off their data, slides, and quarterly sales figures, mercilessly subject-

ing their listeners to bullet-ridden presentations that treat them like the guests of honor at a firing squad.

All right, I'm exaggerating—it's not quite that bloody. Bloodless is more like it.

The point is that dumping information on your listeners is no way to achieve genuine and lasting influence.

So why not be an exciting speaker instead? Here are six questions to ask yourself concerning the people you'll be talking to.[40]

1. **Who** is this audience in terms of maturity, culture, experience, socioeconomic level, and so on? ("Culture" here can mean many things besides nationality or geographic origin. Examples include clubs or social groups, departments within a corporation, religious affiliation, and so on.)

2. **How much** information do your listeners already have? What do you need to give them that someone else hasn't?

3. **What** are their expectations and preferences concerning your presentation? (For example, military personnel probably expect to see a PowerPoint presentation, while leadership teams almost certainly prefer a discussion of the strategic vision rather than operational details, etc.)

4. Is there a clear **emotional climate** (good or bad) regarding this situation that has relevance to your speech? Examples include recent mass layoffs at a company; a just-announced huge increase in sales; the death of a beloved leader; etc. Your audience may be strongly biased toward or against your message based on what they're feeling at the time you speak. If you're a new salesperson talking to a longstanding customer, for instance, are you facing a group of managers with whom the previous rep had a particularly warm relationship? In that case, what might you say that would get you off on the right foot?

5. **Who** has spoken to this audience in the past? What did they speak about? What approach did they use, and was it successful? If not, what might you do differently?

---

40 Note that conducting an audience analysis such as this one precedes putting together the content of your presentation. As stated above: How do you know *what* you should be telling these people until you know *who* they are and what they need?

6. **What else** can your liaison or contact tell you about this audience, the occasion, the personalities involved, or any other relevant information? If you have no contact within a company or organization, a little research on the Internet may pay off handsomely.

By answering these questions, you'll be much better armed as you approach your engagement. You'll then be able to put together content that will give these listeners exactly what they need to hear on this particular occasion.[41]

Proceed along these lines and you'll not only have a leg up on succeeding with this audience, you'll also have greater confidence ahead of time that you'll be able to do so.

Consider the above questions again. Now **write out a brief audience analysis** for a group you've either presented to in the past or will be speaking to in the future.

AUDIENCE ANALYSIS

_____

_____

_____

_____

_____

_____

_____

_____

_____

_____

_____

_____

_____

_____

_____

41 Remember that speaking occasions are always situational, and even speaking to the same audience at a different time might benefit from a different approach.

EXERCISE 11-3

DECIDING ON YOUR PURPOSE

Good! You've just completed a brief audience analysis. Having done so, you should have a firm grasp of the make-up of your audience including their expectations and preferences.

Now you're ready to give some serious thought to what you'll try to bring about with these listeners—in other words, your purpose in giving this presentation.

"But," you say, "The purpose is obvious! I've been asked to speak about..."

That's exactly the mistake many speakers make: they confuse purpose with topic. Yet the two are very different.

In fact, far too many presentations fail because the speaker has no clear idea of the purpose the speech is intended to achieve.

Your purpose is simply what you want to accomplish in a speech. Purpose should always be phrased using a single active infinitive verb—"to inform," "to persuade," "to motivate," "to entertain," "to reassure," "to energize . . ." followed by the specifics of your topic, this audience, and in this situation.

You might, for instance, state your purpose this way:

> MY PURPOSE: "To excite the sales force about the improvements in customer service we've made that they should share with prospects."

Notice how this gives you a specific and active goal for your presentation: To excite your sales force is different from simply informing them about the changes in customer service. You could talk about these improvements in any number of ways, but if your purpose is to actually excite your salespeople, your approach must have a particular flavor to it.

Note also how your purpose is entirely different from your topic, the improvements in customer service. To give another example, you might be discussing the recent upgrades to a software program that make using it more intuitive for current customers. That's your topic; but your purpose will be to get those customers to realize how their life is about to become much easier.

In other words, your content only exists so that you can accomplish your purpose. This is worlds away from gathering content just because you know about it or you think your audience wants to hear about this particular thing.

Content is information: facts, stories, increases in revenue, reports, deliverables, performance metrics, testimonials, research studies, personal anecdotes and experiences, and any and all other data you'll include in your speech to achieve your purpose. But it's always subordinate to what you're trying to accomplish in giving this speech or presentation.

It's amazing, in fact, how many speakers run around gathering material for a presentation and never once stop to ask: "What am I really trying to accomplish with this audience? What's my true purpose apart from the information I'm about to deliver?"

Take a moment now, and using your audience analysis from Exercise 11-2 above, decide on a **specific purpose** for a past or future presentation to this audience:

MY PURPOSE:

_____

_____

Excellent! You've a) completed an audience analysis and b) decided on a specific purpose for your speech. This process should sharpen your ability to understand your listeners and clarify your reason for speaking to them.

Now it's time to figure out how to move your audience to action.

EXERCISE 11-4

SETTING AN ACTION GOAL

As a speaker, your goal for a speech or presentation is in one sense always the same: to positively influence your audience's thoughts, feelings, or behavior based on what you talk about. Accomplishing these changes among listeners may sound like a difficult task, but really it isn't. It's fully achievable because your audience is helping you every step of the way.

People attend talks, lectures, keynote speeches, business meetings, employee training, product rollouts, and political rallies because they want to be positively influenced. They want their thinking and behavior to be changed. In other words, they're looking for something valuable from you. They would like their time and effort in attending this event to be worthwhile. And they want to go away either knowing more than they did before, or feeling different through a positive change in their lives.

That means, ultimately, that the aim of your presentation is to point people to some positive action. The three elements named in the first paragraph above always go together: When you speak, you should (1) add to listeners' knowledge, (2) get them to feel that what they're hearing is beneficial, and (3) lead them to a positive change in behavior.

A problem arises however, if like many speakers you believe your job is primarily to convey information. Thinking this way can lead to a determination to get your information across no matter what happens . . . and the action step you should be aiming for is completely lost! As you've heard me say elsewhere in this book, the bare delivery of information is among the most boring practices a speaker can inflict on listeners.

So, as a reminder of where real influence lies—and that your audience not information is what matters when you speak—remember this:

> If you truly want to influence people, be clear on the action you want them to take as a result of your speech.

Of course, each speaking situation and every audience is unique, so the timing of that action may differ. For instance, you might be trying to get people to sign a petition before they leave the room (immediate action). Or you might want a prospective business partner to agree to a second meeting concerning a project (intermediate action). Finally, you may be focused on developing a closer relationship with the people you're speaking to today (long-term action).

Whatever the action is, build it into your goals for your speech or presentation!

How to Quantify Success. Including an action goal for an audience is one way to quantify your speaking success. That's important, because public speaking is not always an easily quantifiable situation.

For instance: Did your listeners take the action you were hoping for (short- or long-term) following your speech? Did they indicate that they're open to your ideas? Have they indicated they're considering the steps you've outlined? These are all actions in the sense of changing an audience's thoughts, feelings, or behavior.

WRITING OUT YOUR ACTION GOAL

Let's review the steps you've taken so far in this chapter on setting goals.

(A) You've analyzed your audience so that you understand their needs.

(B) You've decided on your purpose and (in a real speaking situation) gathered material to accomplish that purpose.

Now you're ready to write out an action goal of what you're looking for from these listeners—something you'd like them to think, feel, or do as a result of what you'll say. Once again, use the past or future presentation you've been working with in the last few pages as you write out your action goal.

For instance, one of my clients has a tendency to wave his arms around, push up his shirt sleeves, and otherwise include lots of extraneous movement in the first one or two minutes of a speech. By now, I know about this habit of his, and I understand that it comes from nervousness. As I demonstrated for him the "neutral position" of starting out a speech (arms at one's sides), my action goal was to get him to speak with greater physical stillness and focus.

Now it's your turn:

ACTION GOAL:

_____

_____

It doesn't have to be any longer than that, but it has to be there!

EXERCISE 11-5

CHECKLISTS FOR MEASURING YOUR PROGRESS

Below are checklists for measuring your progress as you continue to develop and grow as a speaker. Many of the approaches and techniques already covered in this book are included, along with some others. Together, these items constitute measurable elements of successful speaking—a goal towards which you should continually aspire.

From the subject groups below, check off in the box to the LEFT each skill you'd like to acquire or improve. As you achieve that skill, check off the box to the RIGHT under "Accomplished." Then go on to another skill you haven't yet acquired or mastered.

You needn't follow the order of items as they're listed below. Feel free to focus on any skill you're interested in improving at any particular time. In this way, you'll be measuring your progress step-by-step with an appropriate action, just as we discussed above concerning influencing audiences. You'll also see that next to some groups of skills is the chapter in parentheses where you can review information already covered in this book.

THE CHECKLISTS

POSITIVE COPING STATEMENTS (CHAPTER TWO)

SKILL	ACCOMPLISHED	
○	○	I understand that I have all the skills necessary to be a good speaker.
○	○	I believe that my audience wants to hear this speech.
○	○	I know that people don't always show their interest in their faces.
○	○	I accept that my worst fears are really not going to happen.
○	○	Irrational fears have no basis in reality.
○	○	One bad speech or presentation is not that critical. It's a small thing.
○	○	I've learned not to ignore my positive achievements when I speak.
○	○	My presentation will not be perfect. No one's ever is.
○	○	Overcoming speech anxiety is a courageous act. Some people hide!
○	○	I'll never please everybody, so I won't worry about doing so.

RELAXATION AND FOCUS (CHAPTER THREE AND CHAPTER FIVE)

SKILL	ACCOMPLISHED	
○	○	Learn the progressive relaxation technique.
○	○	Practice the "mini-vacation" exercise.
○	○	Breathe diaphragmatically.
○	○	Slow down my breathing and make it deeper.
○	○	"Follow my breath" or "Listen to the breath."
○	○	5-5-5 count: inhalation, pause, exhalation.
○	○	"Listen" passively and let intrusive thoughts drift on their way.

MINDFULNESS (CHAPTER FIVE)

SKILL	ACCOMPLISHED	
○	○	Practice focused relaxation.
○	○	I stay "present" rather than living in the past or the future.
○	○	I've learned how to enjoy the moment even when doing chores.
○	○	I observe and contemplate the miracle of even ordinary things.
○	○	There is rarely any need to hurry.
○	○	I think 'I will now point at myself,' and then I point away from me.

PERFORMANCE SKILLS (CHAPTER FOUR AND CHAPTER SIX)

SKILL	ACCOMPLISHED	
○	○	I smile more when I speak in public.
○	○	I create a communication bond with my audience.
○	○	Eye contact is easy, and keeps me connected with my listeners.
○	○	I command my performance space, taking up as much as I need.
○	○	I gesture naturally at important points, and my gestures are strong.
○	○	I carry myself like a person worth listening to.
○	○	My relationship is with my listeners, not PowerPoint.
○	○	I pay close attention to whether my audience receives my message.

VOCAL DYNAMICS (CHAPTER SEVEN)

SKILL	ACCOMPLISHED	
○	○	I know how to belly breathe, and I practice it!
○	○	I speak from my center, where my power originates.
○	○	I vary my pitch and vocal expressiveness so I'm interesting to listen to.
○	○	I pause after key points. Also in transitions. And some more.

POSITIVE VISUALIZATION (CHAPTER EIGHT)

SKILL	ACCOMPLISHED	
○	○	I think in terms of communication rather than performance.
○	○	Speaking dynamically will clearly help my career and customers.
○	○	I know how to "turn the hot spotlight" around. OR
○	○	The light is shining from within me and reaching my listeners.
○	○	I run my "Command Performance Movie" in my head for success.

TOUGH LOVE (CHAPTER NINE)

SKILL	ACCOMPLISHED	
○	○	I've learned how to get over myself when I speak!
○	○	This speech or presentation isn't about me.
○	○	People really don't care about me—they are here for their benefit.
○	○	I'm no longer narcissistic but thoroughly professional.

TIME MANAGEMENT AND PREPARATION

SKILL	ACCOMPLISHED	
○	○	I analyze my audience: demographics, needs, and expectations.
○	○	Enough time for adequate research helps me prepare.
○	○	An outline helps me shape my speech.
○	○	A PREPARATION OUTLINE contains complete thoughts.
○	○	NOTES WITH KEY WORDS ONLY is for the actual speech.
○	○	I practice 3-5 times while using my notes.

PHYSICAL PREPARATION

SKILL	ACCOMPLISHED	
○	○	Some butterflies and nerves are normal, and help psyche me up.
○	○	I know how to "ground" my feet for steadfastness and flexibility.
○	○	Like an athlete in training, I pay attention to diet, exercise, and rest.
○	○	I build in "quiet time" on the day of my performance.

OBSERVATION OF OTHER SPEAKERS

SKILL	ACCOMPLISHED	
◯	◯	I attend at least three speeches or presentations per month.
◯	◯	Rating speakers' presence helps sharpen my awareness.
◯	◯	Categories include organization, logic, and supporting evidence.
◯	◯	I also rate use of voice, stance, movement, and gestures.
◯	◯	The speaker's emotional effect on the audience also matters!

12

CURTAIN CALL! LEARNING TO LOVE SPEAKING IN PUBLIC

When you began reading this book you were in very good company concerning the debilitating fear known as *glossophobia*.

Between 70 and 75 percent of Americans report a fear of public speaking.[42] As of the last official census on April 1, 2010, the population of the United States was 308,745,538.[43] If one out of every ten speech fright sufferers experiences truly serious speaking anxiety, that adds up to nearly 22,000,000 Americans with this problem.

That's twenty-two *million*.

And then there's the rest of the world.

If you've practiced the exercises and visualizations in these pages, however, you should now be much better prepared to cope with your speaking fear and therefore to succeed as a speaker. Specifically, a) you should have a better understanding of what causes speech fright, b) own a "toolbox" of tools

42 Karen Kangas Dwyer, *Conquer Your Speechfright* (Fort Worth: Harcourt Brace, 1998), 3-12, citing McCroskey, 1993; and Richmond & McCroskey, 1995.

43 http://2010.census.gov/news/releases/operations/ cb10-cn93.html. Accessed March 2, 2011.

and techniques you can use to cope with fear when it strikes, and c) possess more confidence as a result of a) and b).

You're also much better informed than the general population. You know, for instance, how to be a mindful and focused presenter who can visualize success and actually make it happen.

It's time to take your new knowledge and skills and apply them to the limitless world of influential public speaking. Your effectiveness as a speaker and your enjoyment of the process should continue to grow from this point forward.

A NEW WORLD OF SPEAKING INFLUENCE

As of today, you have a specific mission as a speaker and presenter. Most formal presentations across the globe range from mediocre to painful. It's your job in your small but meaningful way to change that situation for the better.

Even after many years as a singer, actor, professor, presentation coach, and speech consultant, I remain in awe of the difference an outstanding talk or lecture can make in people's lives. Public speaking remains one of the most exciting experiences in modern society. Real influence can occur when one human being speaks with knowledge and passion to an interested audience: a changing of thoughts, feelings, and actions that simply cannot be reproduced in any other way. It's as though an electric spark jumps from the stage to the audience when the presentation begins. And when it is done right, that audience is galvanized.

We give speeches to influence *people*—and the best opportunity to do so is to be in their presence, with our full humanity on display. To understand this opportunity—and not to treat a speech as a pro forma exercise in information delivery—is to become enlivened and energized about speaking in public. In few other ways are we allowed to affect other people's thoughts and behavior so profoundly.

One of the worst aspects of public speaking anxiety is that it divorces us from this reality. Focused on our fears, we lose sight of our listeners' needs and our ability to fulfill those needs. Worst of all, we may even run from the opportunity to do so. Ultimately, then, the value of books like this one is to point toward the door of influence that can open through speaking, a door that speech anxiety sufferers have nailed shut.

There's a world of public speaking enjoyment beyond that door. *Enjoyment.* If this book has pried away a plank or two so you can see daylight, then it has done its job.

APPENDIX

HALTING A PANIC ATTACK JUST BEFORE YOU SPEAK

Clients sometimes ask me for a trick they can use to keep from panicking or freezing just before they're about to speak. I don't believe there are any tricks to becoming a more confident speaker. Each of us must be willing and eager to talk to listeners about a topic we're passionate about and want others to know. Put simply, there is no comparison between communicating honestly with an audience and trying to put something over on them.

Leave that to conjurers.

What I offer these clients instead are the five techniques listed below. These are quick-fixes that can be remarkably effective in those last few moments before you speak, which is of course when you need them most if you're about to panic.

Each of these techniques has been explained previously in these pages. Here, however, are shorthand versions. Photocopy the following page. Keep it with you if you find yourself longing to sprinkle magic dust over yourself to instantly gain speaking confidence!

BEFORE YOU DO ANYTHING, START TO BREATHE

MORE SLOWLY AND DEEPLY.

1. SINGLE POINT: Focus on making the various areas in your awareness a *single point*: What's the ONE THING you want to say to this group? Now marshal all your resources into connecting with these listeners and saying it.

2. OPEN THE EMOTIONAL GATE: Accept the situation you're in and open up to it. Closing yourself off emotionally—blocking your emotions—is making you fragile and brittle. Become *present*, part of this moment. Live it and enjoy it!

3. FACIAL RELAXATION/ANIMATION: Allow your face to go completely slack, devoid of any animation, lifeless. (Do this privately, of course.) Now allow your personality to flow back into your face. You should feel relaxed and energized after your brief "rest."

4. GROUND YOURSELF: Place your feet flat on the floor at shoulder-width, with your weight distributed evenly. Feel the power of the earth beneath you. You yourself are steadfast and powerful.

5. MOVE! Find an excuse to move: a last-minute task, a person to speak to, a visit to the bathroom, or checking arrangements on stage. "Embodied cognition," says movement itself will help you think. You'll also dissipate nervous energy.

INDEX

The **Genard** Method

PERFORMANCE-BASED
PUBLIC SPEAKING TRAINING

The *Fearless Speaking* system is a core component of The Genard Method of performance-based public speaking training. This method created by Dr. Genard is the result of over thirty-five years of applying theatrical techniques to the world of oral communication. His unique approach has

inspired professionals worldwide in speaking for leadership, improving their voice and speech, delivering executive-level presentations, and overcoming speech anxiety.

To learn more about how The Genard Method can help you take your life and career to the next level, please visit:

www.GenardMethod.com

Join us online!

The **Genard** Method

PERFORMANCE-BASED
PUBLIC SPEAKING TRAINING

Stay current on dynamic communication skills by joining our online community. Visit www.GenardMethod.com. Access ongoing content and learning resources. Continue your journey of speaking with confidence!

Receive Dr. Gary Genard's blog *Speak for Success!* along with his monthly e-newsletter, Insights articles, podcasts, and other free content. Dr. Genard's publications include books, e-books, and learning guides on a wide range of topics for improved public speaking.

How to Give a Speech
A fast-paced guide to more dynamic speeches and presentations. Learn 75 "quick-tips" for gaining confidence and influence. For novice to seasoned speakers. Available in paperback and e-book.

e-books — Dr. Genard's insights on topics of interest to all speakers
- *12 Easy Ways to Achieve Presence and Charisma*
- *How to Start a Speech*
- *Positive Visualization to Reduce Speech Anxiety*
- *Body Language to Look and Feel Confident*

Learning Guides — Includes performance-based exercises for improved public speaking skills
- *Convince Listeners through the Power of Your Voice*
- *How to Use Body Language and Gestures as a Speaker*

Join us online!